AN ESSAY ON NEGATION

THE ITALIAN LIST

Paolo Virno

AN ESSAY ON NEGATION

FOR A LINGUISTIC
ANTHROPOLOGY

TRANSLATED BY LORENZO CHIESA

CALCUTTA LONDON NEW YORK

Questo libro è stato tradotto grazie ad un contributo alla traduzione assegnato dal Ministero degli Affari Esteri e della Cooperazione Internazionale Italiano

This book has been translated thanks to a contribution awarded by the Ministry of Foreign Affairs and International Cooperation of Italy

The Italian List

SERIES EDITOR: **Alberto Toscano**

Seagull Books, 2018

Originally published as Paolo Virno, *Saggio sulla negazione. Per una antropologia linguistica* © 2013 Bollati Boringhieri editore, Turin

English translation © Lorenzo Chiesa, 2018

First published in English translation by Seagull Books, 2018

ISBN   978 0 8574 2 438 9

British Library Cataloguing-in-Publication Data

A catalogue record for this book is available from the British Library

Typeset by Seagull Books, Calcutta, India

Printed and bound by Maple Press, York, Pennsylvania, USA

CONTENTS

1.

Mirror Neurons and the Faculty of Negation

1.1

LOGIC AND ANTHROPOLOGY

Ever since its beginnings and at each of its turns, the investigation of linguistic negation has always been an anthropological investigation. Explaining the main characteristics and uses of the sign 'not' means explaining some of the distinctive traits of our species: the capacity to detach oneself from surrounding events and psychic drives; the alternation between inhibitions and disinhibitions that are not prescribed by strategies of environmental adaptation; the need for rituals and institutions; the ambivalence of affects; the propensity to suddenly transform our most habitual behaviours. The linguist and the logician fully become anthropologists, unintentional epigones of Arnold Gehlen and Claude Lévi-Strauss, when they discuss the value to be attributed to a double negation ('I am *not* saying that I do *not* love you'), or the unbridgeable gap that separates contradictory statements ('*x* is sweet' / '*x* is *not* sweet') from contrary ones ('*x* is sweet' / '*x* is bitter'). That is, they fully become anthropologists during their hard work on syntactic and semantic problems, not simply by chitchatting at lunch break. Wittgenstein used to say that at times a whole treatise of philosophy is condensed into a drop of grammar. This is in the first place the case with the cumuliform cloud that is the grammar of the 'not': it is possible to obtain from it some information about the way in which the *Homo sapiens* primate is in the world, as well as a key to decipher the set of feelings and behaviours that make us speak—depending on our inclinations—of the discontent of civilization or of the actuality of revolution.

In this prologue, which is in many ways akin to a theatre rehearsal that prepares the staging of the play on the programme, I would like to indicate without hesitation the ethical and political implications of a study concerning the common faculty of saying how things are *not*. These implications are also present, and possibly most visible, in the dispassionate analysis of texts by Plato and Frege that we will encounter later on. In order to give the right emphasis to the role that the logical connective 'not' plays in the human form of life, I propose three related hypotheses on the social, or rather public, disposition of our mind. To be more precise: three hypotheses whose theme is the singular discontinuity between the biological foundation of this sociality and its tortuous linguistic developments, marked as they are by the telluric power of negation.

Hypothesis I

The human animal understands the intentions and emotions of other human animals due to an original intersubjectivity that precedes the very constitution of individual subjects. The 'we' proves its worth even before the self-conscious 'I' comes to the fore. The relation between members of the same species is, first of all and especially, an impersonal relation. Thinkers such as Lev Vygotsky, D. W. Winnicott and Gilbert Simondon[1] have insisted on the existence of a field of pre-individual experience. Vittorio Gallese, one of the scientists credited with the discovery of mirror neurons, has reformulated this question in a particularly incisive way, anchoring the priority of the 'we' over the 'I' to the functioning of a specific area of the brain. In order to know that somebody is suffering or enjoying, looking for shelter or trouble, is about to attack or kiss us, we do not need propositions, not to mention any baroque attribution of intentions to the mind of the other. The activation of a group of neurons located in the ventral part of the inferior frontal lobe is more than enough.

---

1 Lev Vygotsky, *Thought and Language* (Cambridge MA: MIT Press, 1986[1934]); Donald Woods Winnicott, *Playing and Reality* (London: Tavistock, 1971); Gilbert Simondon, *L'individuation psychique et collective* (Paris: Aubier, 1989).

Hypothesis II

Language is not in the least a powerful echo chamber for this preliminary sociality, shared by all anthropomorphic primates. It would be wrong to suppose that language amplifies and articulates with an abundance of means the harmony of the minds that is already guaranteed by the cerebral apparatus. Verbal thought instead causes the weakening, or even the temporary breakdown, of this *co-feeling* [*cosentire*],[2] which is responsible for the immediate comprehension of the actions and passions of another human animal. Far from corroborating neuro-physiological empathy, the mastery of syntax hinders and at times suspends it. Language differs from communicative codes based on traces and signals, as well as from silent cognitive operations (sensations, mental pictures, etc.), because it is able to *negate* every kind of representation. Even the perceptual evidence that makes us say 'This is a man' when facing an immigrant ceases to be incontrovertible as soon as it is subjected to the work of the 'not'. The failure of reciprocal recognition between members of the same species is rooted in language. The statement 'This is not a man' is grammatically impeccable, provided with a sense and can be uttered by anyone. The speaking animal alone has the capacity to *not* recognize his neighbour.

Hypothesis III

Language does not fail to provide an antidote to the poison it has injected into the innate sociality of the mind.

---

2 See Franco Lo Piparo, *Aristotele e il linguaggio. Cosa fa di una lingua una lingua* (Rome: Laterza, 2003), p. 28ff.

In addition to partly or wholly sabotaging the empathy produced by the mirror neurons, it offers a remedy (or better, the only adequate remedy) to the damages it has thus caused. The initial sabotage can in turn be sabotaged. The public sphere, which is the ecological niche of our actions, is the unstable result of a laceration and a suture, where the former is no less important than the latter. It therefore resembles a scar. In other words: the public sphere is originated by the *negation of a negation*. I am sorry if some readers will be repelled by the dialectical tone of this phrase; there's nothing I can do about it. To avoid any misunderstanding, it is worth adding that the negation of negation does not reinstate a primitive and pre-linguistic harmony. The risk of non-recognition is always eluded or neutralized anew; however, it is also irreversibly inscribed in social interaction.

1.2
IN THE BEGINNING WAS THE 'WE':
AN INTERSUBJECTIVITY WITHOUT SUBJECTS
COROLLARIES TO HYPOTHESIS I

In 'Neuroscienza delle relazioni sociali' [Neuroscience of Social Relations], Gallese writes:

> Approximately ten years ago, our team discovered in the brain of monkeys a population of premotor neurons that are activated not only when the monkey carries out actions that are completed manually (e.g. grabbing an object), but also when it observes the same actions being carried out by

another individual (man or monkey). We have named these neurons 'mirror neurons'.[3]

The experiment has been successfully extended to our species. Mirror neurons have also been observed in the human brain: more precisely, they are located in the ventral part of the inferior frontal lobe which is constituted by two areas, 44 and 45, both belonging to the Broca area. When we see a protester performing some action at the entrance of Goldman Sachs headquarters, which will be reported by the newspapers, '[T]he same neurons are summoned to fire in our brain as those that would fire if it were we ourselves performing that action.'[4] This is the process that allows us to identify without hesitation the emotional moods of a member of our species, as well as to infer the goal its gestures aim at.

Mirror neurons are the biological foundation of the sociality of the mind. I understand a man crying before me because I mimic his behaviour on a cerebral level, that is, because my own lachrymal glands begin to be innervated. This automatic and non-reflective co-feeling is called by Gallese 'embodied simulation'. The interactions of a bodily organism with the world are radically *public*, and are always shared by the other members of the species. Intersubjectivity, which long precedes the operations carried out by individual self-conscious subjects, cannot be

---

3 Vittorio Gallese, 'Neuroscienza delle relazioni sociali' in Francesco Ferretti (ed.), *La mente degli altri. Prospettive teoriche sull'autismo* (Rome: Editori Riuniti, 2003), p. 31.

4 Francesco Napolitano, *Lo specchio delle parole. Su alcuni principi storici e filosofici di psicoanalisi* (Turin: Bollati Boringhieri, 2003), p. 62.

explained by means of the cognitive models used by these subjects:

> Much of what in our interpersonal relations we attribute to the activity of a supposed capacity to formulate theories about the other's mind actually derives from mechanisms that are far less 'mentalistic'. That is, it results from the capacity to create a 'we-centric' space shared with others. The creation of this shared space is the result of the activity of an 'embodied simulation'. This is in turn defined in sub-personal terms by the activity of the mirror neurons that allow us to map onto the same nervous substrate performed actions and observed actions, as well as those feelings and emotions that are personally experienced and those which are observed in others.[5]

The individuation of a 'we-centric space'—where the pronoun 'we' does not indicate a plurality of well-defined 'selves' [*io*] but designates a set of pre-individual or 'sub-personal' relations—is the philosophically crucial point made by Gallese. The same point was also highlighted, using other arguments and a different terminology, by the Russian psychologist Vygotsky and by the English psychoanalyst Winnicott. For Vygotsky, rather than constituting a solid presupposition, the individual mind is the final outcome of a process of differentiation that takes place in collective praxis: 'The true direction of the development of thinking is not from the individual to the social, but from the social to the individual.'[6] According to

---

5 Gallese, 'Neuroscienza delle relazioni sociali', p. 13.

6 Vygotsky, *Thought and Language*, p. 36.

Winnicott,[7] in the first months of life there prevails an intermediate zone in-between the self and the non-self (the zone in which so-called transitional phenomena are grounded): this zone does not link two already established entities (the subject and the object; person x and person y); rather, it makes possible their subsequent formation as distinct polarities. The relation therefore pre-exists the correlated terms. The no man's land between the self and the non-self examined by Winnicott and the 'we-centric space' marked on Gallese's maps do not amount to an ontogenetic interlude which we then leave behind, but to the permanent precondition for social cooperation: 'The interpersonal space in which we live from our birth onwards continues to constitute a substantial part of our semantic space for the duration of our life.'[8] Here, it is not my intention to scrutinize this surprising convergence between very different authors. Still, let us consider it the symptom of an objective theoretical necessity.

Gallese's hypothesis is condensed in a very challenging statement: 'The absence of a self-conscious subject does not preclude [. . .] the constitution of a primitive "self/other" space, and thus characterises *a paradoxical form of intersubjectivity without a subject*.'[9] This statement breaks with an egocentric (or better, solipsistic) conception of simulation, according to which the human animal would generally project onto other minds what he has learnt from his. The 'embodied simulation' Gallese speaks about takes place independently of the intervention of minds

---

7 Winnicott, *Playing and Reality*, p. 179ff.
8 Gallese, 'Neuroscienza delle relazioni sociali', p. 42.
9 Ibid., p. 16 (emphasis added).

capable of learning and generalizing. The great merit of such a position is that it gets rid of several superfluous conceptual entities: the historian of philosophy would see it as an authentic Occam's razor. It is totally incongruous to ascribe to verbal language that immediate intra-species empathy established by the mirror neurons even in 'the absence of a self-conscious subject'. Faced with the behaviours of our neighbours, 'we are almost never engaged in a process of *explicit and deliberate interpretation*'; that is to say, it is not necessary to translate sensory information into 'a series of mental representations that share with language the same propositional format'.[10] But what is even more incongruous is introducing a legion of—post-neural and pre-linguistic—phantom concepts located halfway between mirror neurons and verbal language, which are unable to account for both a cerebral simulation and a proposition. Gallese gives everyone his due: what is neurophysiologic to neurophysiology; what is linguistic to linguistics. In so doing, he makes life difficult for illegitimate pretenders. For example, in order to explain social interaction, it is not at all necessary to postulate that, thanks to its possession of a rudimentary 'theory of the mind', the human animal spends its time representing the representations of others. As Gallese has it:

> If, while sitting at a restaurant, I see someone reaching for a cup of coffee, I will immediately realise that this person is about to sip that drink. The crucial point is: How do I do that? According to the classical cognitivist approach, I would have

---

10 Ibid., p. 25.

to translate the movements of my neighbour into a series of mental representations concerning his *desire* to drink coffee, his *belief* about the fact that the cup he is about to grab is indeed full of coffee, his *intention* to bring the cup to his mouth and drink [. . .]. I think that this account, according to which our capacity to interpret the intentions behind the behaviour of others is exclusively determined by meta-representations that are created by ascribing propositional attitudes to others, is wholly implausible from a biological point of view.[11]

1.3

THIS IS *NOT* A MAN

COROLLARIES TO HYPOTHESIS II

Human sociality and that of other animal species are united by the functioning of mirror neurons. We still need to ask what separates them. Gallese writes: 'The considerable amount of neuroscientific data I have so far summarized suggests that there is a *basic level* of our interpersonal relations that does not make explicit use of propositional attitudes.'[12]

I agree with that. But what are the consequences of embedding language into this 'basic level'? Do propositional attitudes (believing, doubting, postulating, presupposing, etc.) support and enhance the simulation achieved by the mirror neurons? Or do they unsettle it and limit its

---

11 Ibid.

12 Ibid., p. 42.

range? I would definitely choose the second option. I do not doubt the existence of a 'basic level' of sociality—of course, provided it is anchored to neurophysiology and nothing else. On the other hand, I find it unlikely that verbal thought would limit itself to embellishing and refining the 'we-centric space' already delineated by mirror neurons. I rather believe that language destructively retroacts on this space, undermining its solidity. The sociality of the human mind is modelled precisely by such a retroaction. That is to say: it is certainly modelled by the intertwining of neural co-feeling and verbal thought, but also by the lasting tension and the recurring divergence between them.

Any naturalist thinker needs to account for a matter of fact: the linguistic animal is able *not* to recognize another linguistic animal as his neighbour. The most extreme cases, from cannibalism to Auschwitz, are a virulent testament to this permanent possibility. It usually manifests itself by intermediate degrees, inserting itself in mitigated and allusive ways in the gaps of everyday communication. Although it lies at the limits of social interaction, the risk of non-recognition has, nonetheless, implications for its ordinary progress and permeates its entire structure.

What does it mean not to recognize our fellow human being? The old Jew is gnawed by hunger and cries out of humiliation. The Nazi officer knows what this member of his species feels by means of an 'embodied simulation', that is, 'the basic capacity to model the behaviour of the *other* by using the same neural resources used to model *our* behaviour'.[13] But he is able to deactivate, at least partially or provisionally, the empathy generated by mirror neurons. In this way, he manages to treat the old Jew as a non-man. It is far too easy to attribute the atrophy of intra-specific co-feeling to specific historical, cultural and political reasons. The naturalist is always ready to emphasize the invariant characteristics of our species; he cannot suddenly dress the part of the relativist hermeneutician when it most suits him. No three-card tricks, please! It goes without saying that the political-cultural dimension, characterized by an intrinsic varia-bility, has a preponderant influence on the existence of every human being. Yet what matters is bringing into focus the biological basis of this dimension and its variability.

The Nazi officer is able not to recognize the old Jew by virtue of a prerequisite of the primate *Homo sapiens* that is entirely natural (and hence innate and invariant). That is, he is able not to recognize him because the social-ity of *Homo sapiens* is not only forged by mirror neurons but also by language and the syntax that regulates it. If those neurons 'allow us to map onto the same nervous substrate [. . .] feelings and emotions that are personally experienced and those which are observed in others',[14] on the other hand, propositional attitudes authorize us to put into brackets and contradict the representation of the other 'as a person similar to us'.[15] The suspension of neural co-feeling is closely linked to the most relevant feature of human discourses: *negation*, the use of the 'not', the many

13 Ibid.
14 Ibid., p. 15.
15 Ibid., p. 25.

ways in which a speaker can confine a phrase or a whole statement to the region of falsity, error and inexistence.

If we do not lapse into metaphorical or simply meaningless uses of the term (for which even a punch would in a way negate), negation is a function that belongs exclusively to verbal activity. I do not negate what is black by indicating what is white. I negate it if and only if I *say* 'not black'. The distinctive trait of linguistic negation (the adjective is here pleonastic) amounts to proposing again one and the same semantic content with an opposite algebraic sign. The 'not' is added to a predicate phrase ('is kind', 'has gone to Rome', 'loves me') that continues to express in all its consistency the state of affairs or fact of which we speak. The state of affairs or fact are in any case designated, and thus *preserved* as meanings, at the same time as they are verbally *suppressed* ('is not kind', 'has not gone to Rome', 'does not love me'). Let us suppose the SS officer thinks the following: 'The tears of this old Jew are not human.' His clause both preserves *and* suppresses the empathy raised by the 'embodied simulation': it preserves it, since he is anyway speaking about the tears of a member of the same species, and not about a moisture like any other; he suppresses it, by taking away from the tears of the old man that human characteristic which, however, was implicit in their immediate perception-designation as 'tears of an old man'. It is only thanks to this tendency to repudiate what is nonetheless admitted that the sign 'not' can destructively interfere with the 'sub-personal' biological apparatus that is our neural co-feeling. Negation certainly does not prevent the mirror neurons from being activated, but it makes their meaning ambiguous and their effects reversible. The Nazi officer does not have any difficulty in considering the old Jew a 'non-man', even if he fully understands his emotions and intentions through a simulating identification. Demonstrating a noteworthy expertise in ruining intra-species empathy, verbal thought constitutes the condition of possibility of what Kant called 'radical evil'.

Hypothesis II allows us to read in an unusual way one of the most enlightening and suggestive texts that have ever been written on the social mind: Section A of the fourth chapter of Hegel's *Phenomenology of Spirit*,[16] which is in fact dedicated to the reciprocal recognition of self-consciousness. It is widely believed that these pages contain a happy-end story, that is, that they illustrate the way in which—having overcome many dramatic obstacles—reciprocal recognition is in the end achieved. I think this is a misunderstanding. If we browse through the fourth chapter of *Phenomenology* without prejudice (perhaps hiding Hegel's book behind Steven Pinker's latest work, to avoid making a bad impression), we soon become aware that it accounts instead for the different ways in which reciprocal recognition between linguistic animals can *fail*. Hegel presents a long list of impasses and empty gestures: as aggressiveness that destroys empathy and drags us towards general self-destruction; the slave's unilateral recognition of the master; the gradual emancipation of the enslaved non-man, who then in turn stops recognizing as a man the one who previously did not recognize him; last but not least, in a sort of sarcastic

---

16 Georg Wilhelm Friedrich Hegel, *Phenomenology of Spirit* (Oxford: Oxford University Press, 1977[1807]), pp. 111–19.

completion of the whole itinerary, the 'unhappy consciousness' who internalizes the negativity inherent to social relations, up to the point of turning aporia and inconclusiveness into a chronic mode of being. Advancing this series of blatant failures, Hegel shows how the living entity that thinks with words destabilizes the innate harmony between members of the same species, and hence the work of mirror neurons, in some cases even entirely obliterating it. Even if it immediately intuits the frame of mind and intentions of its fellow on the basis of a neurophysiologic process, the human animal is nevertheless able to *negate* that this person is its fellow. The constant threat of non-recognition: this is the Hegelian contribution to a naturalist, yet far from idyllic, investigation of *Homo sapiens'* species-specific sociality.

Among the conceptual and empirical studies one should develop on the basis of *Hypothesis II*, the one that stands out for its importance is that concerning linguistic negation. There are few modern logicians who have openly discussed the status of the 'not', rather than considering it as a primitive sign whose genesis we cannot say anything about. As for linguists, I am convinced that a useful key to clarify the profile of negation as a natural phenomenon is provided by an author who, on top of being denigrated by contemporary naturalistic philosophers, never speaks of negation: Ferdinand de Saussure. I will later dwell on his unexpected contribution (see Chapter 2). Promising materials can also be found in the investigations of experimental psychologists and in some cornerstones of traditional metaphysics. With regard to the former, I limit myself to recalling the study on the 'relations between affirmations and negations' in infant thought carried out by Jean Piaget and his collaborators.[17] With regard to the latter, the stronghold to be conquered is still Plato's *Sophist*.

I believe that the theoretical epicentre of this dialogue, namely, the very dense discussion of the conditions that enable us to negate what is and affirm what is not, meticulously describes an *ontogenetic stage*. In this dialogue, the radical change caused in the first years of life by the grafting of verbal language onto previous forms of thought is reconstructed in all its details (see Chapter 4). The possibility of negating, of stating what is false, of entertaining lively relations with non-being, is not taken for granted but, rather, instigates genuine wonder and poses ticklish questions: 'The fact we can say something that is not true—[this has] always been and still [is] deeply involved in perplexity.'[18]

The *Sophist* is perhaps the only philosophical work that takes seriously the traumatic advent of the 'not' in human life. In a certain sense, Plato's dialogue does nothing but interrogate what happens when a child becomes able to yell angrily at his mother, guilty of paying him little attention: 'You are *not* my mother.' The discovery of the faculty of saying what is *not* is decisive for every new speaker: this very faculty determines a caesura with respect to pre-linguistic cognitions, and, to a certain extent, allows us to disregard neural co-feeling.

---

17 Jean Piaget, *Recherches sur la contradiction* (Paris: Presses Universitaires de France, 1973–74).

18 Plato, *Sophist*, 236e1–3. Quotations from Plato and Aristotle have been modified to fit the Italian translations used by Virno. Several English translations have been consulted and incorporated as far as possible. [Trans.]

The fact that the *Sophist* offers a faithful portrayal of an ontogenetic stage is not the only good reason why we should take it into consideration when we discuss the social mind—as naturalists, of course. There is more. For Plato, the negation of an attribute signals that the grammatical subject of a discourse is *different* (*héteron*) from the property attributed to it by that attribute. What is different is not to be confused with what is contrary: 'So, when it is asserted that a negative signifies a contrary, we shall not agree, but admit no more than this—that the prefix "not", the sign of negation, indicates something different from the words that follow, or rather from the things designated by the words uttered after the negative.'[19]

If I say of a teenager that he 'is not beautiful', I am not indirectly affirming that he 'is ugly', but I leave the door open for an undefined set of heterogeneous (*héteroi*) attributes: 'boring', 'weak', 'tall', etc. These further attributes are not incompatible with what is negated, that is, 'beautiful', so much so that in a different discursive context they can even be correlated with it.

The *héteron*, which is really what is at stake in linguistic negation, helps us to understand the dynamics of nonrecognition among human animals. In stating 'this is not a man' about the crying old Jew, the Nazi officer is not maintaining that his victim is the *contrary* of 'man' but that he is something *different* from the usual meaning of this word: for example, 'totally lifeless', 'devoid of any dignity', 'such that he can only express himself through inarticulate laments'. Nobody can claim that the Jew (or the Arab, in

---

19 Ibid., 257c1–3.

the case of somebody like Oriana Fallaci[20]) is located at the antipodes of the attribute 'human', let alone seriously pass him off as a cat or a plant, given that the mirror neurons attest to the fact that the living being in question belongs to our species. Non-recognition is grounded instead on the tendency of the sign 'not' to evoke a *difference* that, being as such potential and undetermined, is at each turn accounted for through some contingent property (for example, the factual behaviour of a malnourished Jew or of an Arab detained in a refugee camp). When the child says to his mother 'You are *not* my mother,' he is actually saying that she *is not* what in another sense she undoubtedly *is*. The child gradually becomes acquainted with the *héteron*, with what is 'different'. The Nazi and Oriana Fallaci display the terrible side of this same acquaintance.

1.4

THE PUBLIC SPHERE AS NEGATION OF A NEGATION

COROLLARIES TO HYPOTHESIS III

Language does not domesticate *Homo sapiens'* aggressiveness but radicalizes it beyond measure, bringing it to that extreme limit that is the *dis*-avowal [*dis-conoscimento*] of our fellow human being. It is undoubtedly legitimate to believe that verbal thought reshapes our innate co-feeling from end to end. But only on condition that we do not omit a thorny specification: 'Reshaping' means first and foremost that verbal thought erodes the original certainty

---

20 Oriana Fallaci (1929–2006): Italian journalist and author. Towards the end of her career she wrote controversial articles and books against Islam. [Trans.]

of co-feeling. Only this erosion, which on its own is lethal, paves the way for a complex and ductile sociality, scattered with pacts, promises, norms, conflicts, institutions that are never stable, and collective projects whose outcomes are imponderable. It would be foolish to believe that a discourse aimed at persuading our interlocutors is the quiet cultural prolongation of the empathy guaranteed from the beginning by the mirror neurons. Nothing is more false. A persuasive discourse is rather a compulsory, and hence itself *natural*, answer to the laceration that linguistic negation has inflicted on neurophysiologic empathy. Our rhetorical reasoning introjects the possibility of saying 'this is not a man' and always blocks its accomplishment anew. It does nothing but deactivate, with words relevant to given circumstances and affects, the partial deactivation of the 'we-centric space' caused by the faculty of speech. References to shared premises (*éndoxa*), individuation of thematic repertoires (*tópoi*), metaphors, litotes, enthymemes, ironies, refutations, polemics: these traditional resources of rhetoric linguistically restrain the violent negativity that language itself has inserted into animal life; they regulate the use of the 'not' and delimit the range of the *héteron*; all in all, they allow the reciprocal recognition of living beings which could also *dis*-avow each other.

The public sphere that is typically human has the logical form of a *negation of negation*. It is a 'not' that is added before the latent phrase 'non-man'. Linguistic negation exercises its power even on itself: the 'not' that suppresses-and-preserves can in turn be suppressed (and preserved as a liminal possibility, liable to be infinitely differed). The 'we-centric space', opened by 'embodied simulation' at the moment of birth, becomes a public sphere not because of its developmental strengthening, but, on the contrary, after the risk-laden impairment that befalls it. The 'we-centric space' and the public sphere are the two similar yet incommensurable ways in which the sociality of the mind is manifested *before* and *after* the experience of linguistic negation. Before this experience, there is the infallible and impersonal neural co-feeling; after it, there is the uncertainty of persuasion, the metamorphosis and crisis of the process of production, the brutality of political conflicts.

In order to qualify the negation of negation thanks to which language inhibits the 'radical evil' that it has itself made possible, I will avail myself of a theological-political tool which has a tormented history: the notion of *katéchon*. This Greek term, which appears in the apostle Paul's *Second Letter to the Thessalonians*, is usually translated as 'force that holds back'. The *katéchon* is the subject or structure that unceasingly postpones and hinders utter destruction: the triumph of the Antichrist, for the theologian; the breakup of the social order, for medieval and modern political thought. So, language is the naturalistic *katéchon* that, favouring the formation of a public sphere (through the application of a 'not' to a previous 'not'), *holds back* the catastrophe of non-recognition. It is however a very singular *katéchon*, since it protects from a catastrophe that, in other ways, it never stops fomenting: here, the antidote is not different from the poison.

Mirror neurons, linguistic negation, and the intermittent status of reciprocal recognition: these are the coexisting yet dissonant factors that define the social mind of our species. Their dialectic disproves any political theory (for example, Noam Chomsky's) that opposes the natural 'creativity of language' to the iniquity and thirst for violence of historically determined apparatuses of power. The fragility of the 'we-centric space', which is indeed to be ascribed to the perturbations that language and its 'creativity' bring with them, must constitute the realistic background of any political movement that aims at a drastic transformation of the current state of affairs. A great and terrible political philosopher, Carl Schmitt, wrote in a clearly sarcastic way that 'radicalism vis-à-vis state grows in proportion to the radical belief in the goodness of man's nature.'[21] It is high time to prove this malicious equation wrong.[22] An accurate analysis of the social mind allows us to ground the 'radicalism vis-à-vis state' and vis-à-vis the capitalist mode of production on the dangerousness of human nature (a dangerousness fed by the polyvalent use of the 'not'), rather than on its imaginary mildness. Anti-capitalist and anti-state political action does not have any positive presupposition to lay claim to. Rather, it is dedicated to experimenting new and more effective ways of negating negation, of appending the 'not' before 'non-man'. Where this experiment is successful, anti-capitalist and anti-state political action embodies a force that holds back, and thus looks like the *katéchon*.

---

21 Carl Schmitt, *The Concept of the Political* (Chicago: University of Chicago Press, 1996[1932]), p. 61.

22 Paolo Virno, *E così via, all'infinito. Logica e antropologia* (Turin: Bollati Boringhieri, 2010), pp. 148–94.

2.

The Money of Language

OF A PECULIAR OMISSION,
AND THE POSSIBILITY OF REMEDYING IT

Ferdinand de Saussure repeatedly claims that in language there are only 'negative facts', but he does not say a word about linguistic negation. He never misses the opportunity to remind us that the value of a sign is solely defined by its 'non-coincidence with the rest', that is, that x is indeed something precisely because it is *not y*, nor z, nor w, etc. Yet, he does not say anything about the sign 'not'. This omission can be explained in various ways, some unsophisticated, others sharp, but all unhelpful for a theoretical investigation. Here is an example of an unsophisticated explanation: Saussure overlooks the 'not' because he is not interested in the logical form of a judgement and, more generally, in the structure of the proposition. As for an example of a sharp explanation: Saussure has to forsake an accurate analysis of negation precisely because, in his view, the latter constitutes the presupposition of every linguistic analysis, an a priori category that we cannot directly account for, the axiom that makes all demonstrations possible provided that it remains undemonstrated. These hypotheses are not only debatable, but, as I have just said, also useless. The only thing that really matters is to ask whether Saussure's works offer the necessary elements that allow us to achieve what these works fail to achieve, namely, clarifying the specific status of the sign 'not'. My answer is affirmative. In other words, it seems to me possible to infer the characteristics of negation as the basic linguistic operator from the Saussurean description of language as a 'complex of eternally negative differences'.[1]

To specify what is at stake, let me add that if this inference turned out to be legitimate and cogent, it would allow us to tackle more perceptively at least two canonical problems of the philosophical tradition. The first concerns the nexus between language and non-being. From Plato's *Sophist* to Heidegger's *What Is Metaphysics?*, the crucial question has been roughly the following: Does non-being already have its own reality which then manifests itself in our discourses thanks to the word 'not'? Or, on the other hand, is non-being instilled in the experience of the human animal only because it is said by the 'not'? The second question, itself a very old one, concerns the

---

1 Ferdinand de Saussure, *Writings in General Linguistics* (Oxford: Oxford University Press, 2006[2002]), p. 153.

hierarchical relation between affirmation and negation. From Aristotle to Austin, we can draw a demarcation line between those who believe that affirmative and negative propositions share the same logical level, and those who instead observe a fundamental asymmetry between the two forms of linguistic expression, claiming that negation always refers to a previous affirmation (whether real or only hypothetical) and thus gives rise to a discourse *on* discourse.[2] In short: Is the 'not' an integral part of the object-language, or does it have a genuine meta-linguistic value? Does it provide information about the world, or does it deal exclusively with the relation between propositions and the world? As is evident, these are drastic conceptual alternatives, that is, theoretical options doomed to exclude one other. Yet I am convinced that if these alternatives are closely examined through the prism of Saussure's considerations on the negative-differential texture of language, they undergo a radical transformation. The concept of negation that can be deduced from these considerations changes the whole picture, obliging us to formulate differently the two canonical questions we just mentioned. In the following pages I would like to show how and why this is the case.

2.2

FERDINAND DE SAUSSURE'S 'INTIMATE THOUGHT'

Let me summarize Saussure's *idée fixe*, the one we all know and that many set aside (or play down) right after

---

2 See Laurence R. Horn, *A Natural History of Negation* (Stanford, CA: CLSI Publications, 2001), pp. 63–79.

celebrating it. Language is nothing else than a collection of virtually unlimited oppositional relations between terms that, importantly, do not have any reality before their reciprocal opposition, or outside of it. 'In language there are only differences,' writes Saussure. But this is not the most significant hypothesis, so much so that very few ancient or modern linguists would hesitate to subscribe to it. What is most significant, even dizzying, is instead the following observation: while 'a difference generally implies positive terms between which the difference is set up', in language, 'there are only differences *without positive terms*.'[3] The absence of entities that are as such consistent separates the study of language from both the natural and historical sciences: 'Whoever enters the realm of language may as well abandon all hope of finding a fitting analogy, earthly or otherwise.'[4] Contrary to what happens in other fields of knowledge, we are not dealing with things between which there is a difference (*a* is not *b*), but with a difference that generates things (*a* becomes something real only because it is not *b*, and vice versa). The negative relation between linguistic facts pre-exists these very facts and in fact establishes them: 'The *different terms* in language, unlike different elements in chemistry, etc., are no more than *defined differences* between terms which would be empty and void of definition without these differences.'[5]

---

3 Ferdinand de Saussure, *Course in General Linguistics* (London: Owen, 1960[1916]), p. 120.

4 Saussure, *Writings in General Linguistics*, p. 154.

5 Ibid., p. 42.

Of course it is no crime not to pay attention to Saussure. But it does not make sense to fiddle around with his work without taking seriously—that is, literally—its most ticklish and interesting point.

Given that any phonological or lexical phenomenon consists solely of a multiplicity of 'nots' (x is not-y, not-w, etc.), it is easy to believe that language forms a whole with negation: 'In essence language rests on oppositions, on a network of wholly negative values which exist only in mutual contrast.'[6] We should nonetheless add that the primary negation at stake here does not coincide with a particular class of signs but presides over the very formation of every single sign. It is not a peculiar characteristic of some propositions but the condition that makes a proposition possible. We could also say that language is the abode of non-being, the only field of experience in which non-being attains an empirical reality. Our enunciations, obviously including affirmative and monosyllabic ones, are the demonstration that non-being *is* in its own way: they thus amount to an ontological proof of the existence of nothingness.

Saussure does not get overly excited. He frankly admits that 'we will *never* penetrate *enough* the purely negative, purely differential, essence of each of these elements of language that we hastily assume to exist.'[7]

What does the phrase 'never enough' precisely mean? It signals the difficulty of coherently developing a knowledge that, being unable to presuppose positively determined phenomena, should only deal with non-being, where

6 Ibid., p. 47.

7 Ibid., p. 42 (emphasis added).

the latter is, however, concerned with the undeniable reality of articulated sound and intersubjective meaning. The urge to escape from this paradox is nearly irresistible, and we 'hastily assume' that the basic particles of language exist independently. The positivity of signs is false by any standard, yet it is one of those *inevitable appearances* that, according to Kant, nourish metaphysics. But the 'never enough' can also refer to the partial impossibility on the part of the linguist to get to the bottom of certain particular problems. I will single out just one example. Even if we courageously acknowledge the negative-differential nature of language, we nonetheless run a risk, namely, that of assigning an autonomous value, that is, a 'positive' or substantial value, to the individual negative-differential relation, as though at least this relation were a solid *matter of fact*, an unquestionable starting point. But this is not the case: each difference between linguistic terms exists only by virtue of . . . its negative-differential relation with another difference. Using a concept dear to Chomsky, we could say that the primary negativity of which the texture of language is made is endowed with the prerequisite of *recursion*: it is applied again and again, that is, to itself, to the results of its previous applications. The principle according to which each linguistic entity is generated by oppositions 'without positive terms' is also valid for the generative oppositions: it is therefore necessary to go back to the opposition between oppositions, and also, recursively, to the opposition from which the opposition between oppositions is derived; and so on, without end. The non-being of language does not allow for any exception: its recursion is one of those aspects that can 'never' be mastered 'enough'.

The *idée fixe* that accompanies all of Saussure's mature writings like a sort of *basso continuo* has elicited ambivalent reactions among his interpreters. The negativity of signs has been held in high esteem as a foundational act of semiology, but, at the same time, it has appeared as an insurmountable obstacle to the discipline's scientific development. Appreciation soon turns into puzzlement. When will it be possible to dialogue with psychology or biology on equal footing if we stress with excessive insistence that there are only 'negative facts' in language? Puzzlement is more than justified. Furthermore, it is Saussure himself who notes that, if linguistics remains faithful to its object, it has no hope of rising to the status of science, given that it cannot claim a field of phenomena existing autonomously: 'Shall we reveal our intimate thought? It may be feared that a precise view of what *langue* is will lead to doubts about the future of linguistics.'[8]

The structuralist tradition has struggled to come to terms with this 'intimate thought'. Most of the time, it remains discretely silent about it, as if it were the nightmare of a hesitant and melancholic individual. In order to avoid 'doubt[ing] about the future of linguistics', the structuralist tradition has done its best to neutralize or blunt Saussure's *idée fixe*. For example, it has considered the 'purely negative essence' of language as a truth that applies only to the formation of signs, and not to their effective functioning: basically, a kind of *big bang* that accounts for the primordial chaos, yet does not explain anything about the well-defined organisms that have

---

8 Ibid., p. 59.

emerged in the course of evolution. Alternatively, the structuralist tradition has reduced this ticklish Saussurean refrain to a much more accommodating postulate: verbal signs have first and foremost a relation among themselves, and only later, by delimiting and qualifying one other, do they connect with states of affairs in the world. But in order to know that individual words draw their meaning from the sentence that contains them, or that the value of symbols entirely depends on their reciprocal inter-action, the writings of Gottlob Frege and Charles Sanders Peirce were already more than enough: Saussure's distinc-tive trait lies rather in his belief that, being nothing in themselves, signs come to existence only thanks to their mutual opposition. Confronted with these and other attempts at neutralizing Saussure's *idée fixe*, which are both comprehensible and counter-productive, we need to ask: Is it possible to safeguard the hypothesis about the negative-differential nature of language in all its radicality without experiencing epistemological distress?

Saussure's 'intimate thought' does not necessarily entail despair and surrender. The crucial point is that 'a precise view of what *langue* is' requires the use of concepts able to account for non-being, or, which amounts to the same, a difference 'without positive terms'. Ever since its beginnings, philosophy has been concerned with non-being. Preoccupied as they are with well-defined states of affairs, the natural and historical sciences do not even mention it. The obligatory conclusion is that there cannot be a *science* of human verbal language, only a *philosophy*. I think this might be a tendentious, yet not illegitimate, way of paraphrasing Saussure's 'intimate thought'. Beginning with those philosophers who are ashamed of themselves, many will object that when it is cut off from science, from its vigorous enquiry into empirical phenomena, philosophy has always been lazy and facile. Such an objection is simply not relevant here, whatever credit we may give it in general: suffices it to say that, in our case, it misses the point. When linguistic signs are at stake, it is precisely empirical phenomena that necessitate the systematic intervention of philosophical categories, namely, those categories that allow us to think the status and prerogatives of non-being. If he did not part ways with the methods of positive science, the Saussurean linguist would remain aloof from the real life of language. That is, he would evidently show disrespect for the (negative) facts he is dealing with—a kind of disrespect, moreover, that is far from 'scientific'. The considerations on non-being as *héteron*, that is, different, expounded in Plato's *Sophist*, as well as those on the circular relation between being and nothingness which open Hegel's *Science of Logic*, are pertinent—and perhaps even indispensable—to understanding the value of a name or the transformation of a phoneme. But the opposite is also the case: Saussure's acknowledgement of the negativity of language allows a more thorough reading of the *Sophist* and of the *Science of Logic*, insofar as it brings to light the phenomenal counterpart or empirical basis of the speculative concepts manifest in those two works.

2.3

NEGATIVE FACTS

Saussure speaks of 'negative things' and 'negative facts'. This is an extravagant terminology for a linguist. We would expect him to define as negative certain specific verbal performances: for example, the proposition 'Socrates is *not* just,' or the adjective 'use*less*', but never things or facts. Matters clear up as soon as we realize that, for Saussure, negativity concerns first and foremost what language *is*, and only then, in a derived way, what language *expresses*. Independently of which discourse is being uttered, the factual (or objective) reality of language is always characterized by the absence of self-consistent terms.

The 'negative facts' on which Saussure dwells should not be confused with the opposition that may emerge between extra-linguistic perceptions, desires or events. For example, they have nothing to do with the contrast between attraction and repulsion, pleasure and displeasure, survival and suicide, white and black. For a simple reason: a non-verbal fact, even when it hinders another fact or annuls it, does not deserve in any way the label of 'negative'. Repulsion is a prominent physical force, no less efficient than attraction; a slap that polemically follows a kiss is an independent action, endowed with a clear impact. It was Kant, in his 'An Attempt to Introduce the Concept of Negative Magnitudes into Philosophy', who amended the error of those who asserted the existence of 'negative facts' beyond properly linguistic experience: 'For negative magnitudes are not negations of magnitudes [. . .] but something truly positive in itself, albeit something opposed to the positive magnitude.'[9] Displeasure 'is not

9 Immanuel Kant, 'An Attempt to Introduce the Concept of Negative Magnitudes into Philosophy' in David Walford (ed.), *Theoretical Philosophy, 1755–1780* (Cambridge: Cambridge University Press, 1992[1763]), p. 209.

merely a lack, but a positive sensation';[10] similarly, on close inspection, demerit and error are positive. Among other things, the 'Attempt' is important because it offers a meticulous catalogue of everything that does not have a point of contact with linguistic negation in the strict sense, let alone with the basic negativity of language taken as a whole, although it has the appearance of opposition and contrariety. Similar to a concave space that delimits a convex one, Kant's text allows us to circumscribe, by way of contrast, the key requirements of both.

According to Saussure, it is reasonable to define a fact as 'negative' if it fully obtains its reality from a relation of opposition with other facts; if it does not pre-exist the opposition but results from it. Language is the only field in which this paradoxical condition is satisfied. Negative facts can thus only be found in language. Incomparable with the different forms of extra-linguistic opposition, the negative facts of which our discourses are composed do not, however, depend on the sign 'not': as we have already observed, they are not the product of a particular linguistic operation but the background to all the operations that a speaker can carry out. It is therefore necessary carefully to distinguish three heterogeneous levels: (1) the physical and psychological (or more broadly non-verbal) events that, endowed with an autonomous subsistence, hinder the unfolding of other events (e.g. repulsion cancelling out the effects of attraction); (2) the 'negative facts' analysed by Saussure, that is, the differences without positive terms on which the value of signs depends (the word x is something only because it is not y, nor w, nor z, etc.);

---

10 Ibid., p. 219.

(3) negation as a specific logical operation (e.g. 'Socrates is *not* just').

What interests us here is the third level, that is to say, the range of action of the sign 'not'. It all depends on establishing which of the previous levels it originates from: Does logical negation prolong and refine the contrast between extra-linguistic events, perceptions and desires, or is it rooted in the preliminary negativity of language? Far from being unimportant, this choice involves considerable consequences on how we understand the functioning of the mind and human nature itself (assuming, of course, that only *Homo sapiens* has the faculty of negation). I have already anticipated my view in the opening lines of this chapter. I claim that there is no genetic link or even vague analogy between the physical and psychological oppositions of which Kant speaks and the negative assertions we use with nonchalance on the most varied occasions. On the other hand, it seems to me very likely that negation arises from the negative-differential nature of language, that is, that the sign 'not' isolates and concentrates in itself an aspect that pervasively characterizes the life of all signs. It is now a matter of understanding how what language *is* (differences without positive terms) is transformed into what language *expresses* (deactivation of a semantic content; denial; contradiction).

2.4

THE DEDUCTION OF THE 'NOT'

Our attempt at bringing into focus the prerogatives of logical negation in the light of Saussure's *idée fixe* is articulated in two steps. First, we need to determine the value of the sign 'not' in the same way that the value of any other sign is determined ('red', 'dog', 'because', 'perhaps', etc.), namely, by drawing from 'a complex of eternally negative differences'. Subsequently (see 2.5), we will try to show how the genesis of the 'not' out of the primary negativity of language explains the way in which it functions within our assertions about the world.

The sign 'not'—exactly like 'red' and 'dog'—is defined by its opposition to all other signs, namely, by not being what they are. And yet the 'not' presents a clearly visible anomaly: it is indeed easy to ascertain that in this case (and only in this case) there is a complete identity between the defining procedure and the value of the defined term. The opposition to other signs is, at the same time, a productive process and a final product: it generates the 'not' but it is also the semantic content of the 'not'. This point becomes intuitively clear if we make fully explicit, through a series of statements, the negative-differential relations that constitute the signified of the little word 'not'. First, we write:

(α) 'not' is *not* 'x', nor 'y', nor 'w', etc.

What matters is the double occurrence of the same term. The 'not', which in general determines the value of signs ('red' is *not* 'x', nor 'y', etc.), figures at the same time here as a sign liable to be determined. The *explanans* is also the *explanandum*. This redundancy, or compression, is the crucial problem posed by negation to those who take Saussure's philosophy of language seriously. The statement (α) suggests the existence of a reciprocal reference, or better, a circular link between the syntactic function and the semantic value of the 'not'. The first time it appears, the 'not' is a lexical unity to which belongs, in

principle, a specific signified; the second time (. . . is not
. . .), it presents itself as a syntactic connective, or, if you
prefer, as a logical operator. But, as I said, these two sides
imply each other. The syntactic 'not', as the hinge of the
negative-differential relation with 'x', 'y', etc., *institutes* the
semantic 'not', and identifies it as an independent term;
in turn, the latter *designates* the negative-differential relation based on the syntactic 'not'. The logical operation
forms the sign that names it. Vice versa, the 'not' as a
lexical unity has as its signified only that opposition
between signs of which it is also the result: that is, it
denotes its own process of formation. The statement (α)
does not account for this latter aspect. It clarifies the role
the negative-differential relation has in determining the
sign of negation, but it does not throw light on the way
in which the sign of negation, as a determined value, designates the negative-differential relation. The signified of
the 'not' is fully illustrated by two other statements, which
are the coherent development of (α). Let us now write:

(β) 'not' is not-'x', not-'y', not-'w', etc.

(γ) 'not' is the non-being of 'x', 'y', 'w', etc.

As we can see, (β) and (γ) are also characterized by a
duplication of the 'not'. In (β), it figures first as a grammatical subject, then as the recurrent part of innumerable
predicates. On the other hand, in (γ), the second occurrence of the 'not' qualifies a single universal predicate
(*non*-being), which, we should note, isolates and abstracts
the negative component of the particular predicates (not-
'x', not-'y', etc.) that are present in (α). But to speak of
subject and predicate is inaccurate, even misleading. Both
in (β) and (γ) the copula 'is' is in fact equivalent to 'means'.

These two statements express the semantic value of the sign of negation. What is at stake is no longer, as in (α), the production of the 'not' by the primary negativity of language but the designation of this negativity by the 'not' that has been produced. It is worth examining more closely the conceptual kernel of (β) and (γ), as well as the derivation of the latter from the former.

The statement (β) constitutes an intermediate link in the chain between the formation of the sign 'not' and the full manifestation of its signified. Yet as an intermediate link, it appears to be incorrect. It would seem more natural to write in its place: 'Not' means something *because* it is not-'x', not-'y', etc. The difference from other signs (being not-'x', not-'y', etc.) is not usually a specific semantic content but, rather, the condition of possibility for the most diverse semantic contents. For example, the term 'red' means something *because* it is not-'x', not-'y', etc., but of course we cannot say that its meaning (a given chromatic shade) *is* not-'x', not-'y', etc. Things change, however, when the 'not' is in question: in its case, the difference between 'because a sign means' and 'what a sign means' is totally inapplicable. The semantic content of negation is indeed difference as such. From this follows that the something meant by the 'not' fully coincides with the mechanism that allows the 'not' and all the other signs to signify. This is precisely what is expressed by (β): 'Not' is, or means, not-'x', not-'y', etc. Far from being incorrect, this statement accounts for a crucial prerogative of negation.

The statement (γ), the most radical and explicit, exclusively revolves around the signified of the sign 'not'. In it, as already in (β), the semantic value of the first 'not' is one with the logical operation carried out by the second 'not', the one placed before an '*x*', '*y*', etc. But in (γ) this logical operation is substantivized through the term 'non-being'. The outcome is the following: 'Not' is, or means, the non-being of '*x*', '*y*', etc. We may perhaps ask whether it is appropriate to substantivize the logical operation that guarantees the negative-differential relations of which language is composed. My answer is that such a step is appropriate, and even necessary, in a single case, namely, when the negative-differential relations become themselves an *object of designation*; when what matters is the semantic value of the word 'not'. The latter denotes the nothingness that all signs harbour, their insubstantiality. Its peculiar signified amounts to the suppression of the semblance of autonomy and positivity with which the most diverse signifieds present themselves. The 'not' means the non-being of '*x*', '*y*', etc., since it leads '*x*', '*y*', etc., back to the play of differences without positive terms from which they are generated, and in so doing it always *indetermines* them anew.

Let me sum up and conclude. Language singles out the 'not' as a sign specialized in expressing the procedure with which it singles out each and every sign. The value of the 'not' lies in designating the 'complex of eternally negative differences' from which any particular linguistic sign emerges. Used to describe and transform the world, as well as to modulate every kind of action and passion, negation refers, first and foremost, to the genesis of signs. Its cognitive and pragmatic performances are never without a self-reflexive tone; they are nourished by it. If this is so, there is no risk in postulating that the philosophical enquiry into negation has always been de facto an enquiry into the way of (not-) being of language.

2.5
A JANUS-FACED SIGN

I would now like to dwell on some properties of linguistic negation, and, more precisely, on those properties that prevent us from assimilating it—or even just comparing it—to the opposition between physical forces, the contrast between perceptions and the conflict between drives. I would like to show how these properties have much in common with the primary negativity of language. The 'not' is amphibious or Janus-faced: on the one hand, it denotes the differences without positive terms on which the formation of verbal signs depends (of course, also including the 'not'); on the other, it enables us to take distance from any meaning pertaining to the (biological, sociohistorical, oneiric, etc.) experience of *Homo sapiens*. But, and this is the crucial point, the second function of the 'not' is only a repercussion of the first. When I say 'this food is *not* sweet,' or 'the woman in the dream is *not* my mother,' I am applying to a given state of affairs a logical operation that concerns, first and foremost, the negative-differential relations underlying all statements. Like one of the famous angels painted by Paul Klee, negation acts in the world with its gaze turned backward, keeping its eyes fixed on the internal life of language.

(a) *Negation shares the same semantic content as its corresponding affirmation.* If this were not the case, rather than negating, we would limit ourselves to opposing a new affirmation to the initial one. Asserting 'that *p*' and asserting 'that not *p*' are two linguistic acts that share the presence of '*p*'. The 'not' is placed before a syntagm that continues to express the fact of which we speak in all its characteristic traits. The fact is at any rate designated, and in this way preserved as meaning, at the very moment in which it is suppressed and put out of play. The link between 'Socrates' and 'being just' remains what it is even when, in 'Socrates is *not* just,' we vehemently contradict it. It goes without saying that such a property excludes extra-linguistic contrasts from the field of negation. When repulsion, considered as a positive force, clashes with attraction, it does not preserve the 'content' of the latter but annuls it, or, if it overwhelms it, replaces it with an alternative 'content'.

(b) *Negation is asymmetrical with respect to affirmation.* This asymmetry, or difference in logical level, is strictly related to property (a). We could say that negation shares the semantic content of affirmation because it does not deal with it, and it does not deal with it because it carries out an operation that is more sophisticated than the description of an entity or fact. With regard to the 'not', Kant's remarks on existence and Frege's remarks on number are entirely pertinent. For Kant, saying that 'Mont Blanc exists' does not in any way enrich the meaning of 'Mont Blanc', which is instead defined by its location, height, the difficulty in climbing it, etc. Existence is not a 'real predicate', given that it does not qualify the object of a discourse but only the 'thought one has of it'.[11] The same

---

11 Immanuel Kant, 'The Only Possible Argument in Support of a Demonstration of the Existence of God' in David Walford (ed.), *Theoretical Philosophy, 1755–1780* (Cambridge: Cambridge University Press, 1992[1763]), p. 118. [Translation modified to fit the Italian translation used by Virno.—Trans.]

applies to number: according to Frege,[12] while something quite specific corresponds to the word 'green' in our representation of a piece of clothing, nothing is added to its description by stating that it is 'one'. Just as in the case of existence and number, negation itself does not interfere with the predicates attributed to a given state of affairs: it neither alters nor disaggregates them. The 'not' concerns exclusively the relation between statements and facts, without modifying in any way the characteristics of the facts of which the statements speak. The property of asymmetry itself helps to trace an insurmountable demarcation line between negation and non-verbal oppositions: two contrasting perceptions are always set on the same logical level; attraction and repulsion are symmetrical.

(c) *Negation does not express what is contrary, but what is different*. When I say 'the wall is not white' and 'this food is not sweet,' I am not claiming, not even implicitly, that the wall is black or the food bitter. As we saw in the first chapter, for Plato negating a predicate means asserting that the object of discourse is 'different' (*héteron*) from the property that the predicate assigns it. We should stress that it is not contrary, but different. To fully grasp the gap between negation ('Mario is *not* good') and the indication of the contrary ('Mario is bad'), it is worth dwelling on cases in which the speaker uses predicates that are devoid of an antipode. There is no concept that is diametrically opposed to 'man', 'substance' or 'yellow'. Unlike 'sweet' or 'good', these terms do not have a contrary. And yet we can negate them without difficulty: '*x* is not a man,' '*y* is

---

12 See Gottlob Frege, *The Foundations of Arithmetic* (Evanston, IL: Northwestern University Press, 1980[1884]).

not a substance,' etc. This means that negation does not *ever* refer to the contrary of the predicate to which it applies: not even when this contrary really exists. Rather, it refers to a difference whose content is undefined, or only potential: 'Is not beautiful' means only 'different from beautiful'. It is almost superfluous to remark that such a difference, which cannot be led back to a relation between contraries, is totally alien to extra-linguistic oppositions.

Negation has the properties we have just examined because it refers, in the first place, to the 'complex of eternally negative differences' from whence the phonological and lexical unities originate. The 'not' behaves like a *commutator*: it transfers the primary negativity of language, of which it is a condensed expression, to discourses on extra-linguistic reality. In other words, it projects onto the relation between propositions and facts what rather characterizes the relation between signs. We should reconsider the three properties from this perspective.

Let us begin with property (a): negation shares the same semantic content as the corresponding affirmation. This sharing is a direct consequence of the original *intralinguistic* function of the sign 'not'. As seen earlier (2.4), this sign refutes the apparent autonomy and positivity of 'dog', 'grass', 'love', etc., referring the values of these terms back to the negative-differential relations that produced them. The 'not' denotes the nothingness inherent to the *same* word that, from another angle, has a well-defined meaning. Within language, being and nothingness are coextensive: 'Dog' is also, at the same time, not-'dog'. In the same way, affirmation and negation are coextensive. In a passage that will leave anyone who has read some

Hegel breathless, Saussure writes: 'Being. Nothing *is*, or at least nothing *is* absolutely (in the linguistic domain) [. . .] The basic form of a judgment "this *is* that" is open to countless criticisms, because of the need to say in relation to what "this" or "that" is identified and determined, no object being naturally bounded or given, and no object evidencing *being*.'[13]

This is one of the very few places in which Saussure extends his thesis on the insubstantiality of signs to the propositional structure, or, rather, to the 'basic form of a judgment'. Given that in language 'nothing *is* absolutely,' the assertion 'this *is* that' contains in itself from the outset the possibility of turning into 'this *is not* that.' An identical semantic content is subjected to affirmation and negation. This principle, first valid 'in the linguistic domain', is then transposed onto judgements on events and affects. In saying 'the woman in the dream is *not* my mother,' we nevertheless refer to the link between 'woman in the dream' and 'being my mother'; we certainly repudiate this link, but do not modify it.

Let us now try to account for property (b), according to which negation is asymmetrical to affirmation. The origin of this asymmetry is obvious. We in fact know that the 'not' is a term specialized in designating the procedure with which language singles out all individual terms. The sign 'not' says something *about* the nature and formation of signs. Because of this reflexive character, it is located on a logical level that is superior to that of words such as 'dog' or 'perhaps', which, in spite of being produced by negative-differential relations, do not refer to them in any

---

13 Saussure, *Writings in General Linguistics*, p. 55.

way. This explains why, when it is active in discourses on empirical experience, negation limits itself to qualifying the relation between propositions and facts yet remains silent on the characteristics of the facts in question. The asymmetry between the 'not' and other signs extends itself into the asymmetry between negation and the semantic content of the proposition in which it appears.

Finally, property (c): negation does not express what is contrary but what is different. This property derives from the fact that the 'not' represents first and foremost the differences *without positive terms* that define the value of signs. Now, it is evident that, in the case of contraries, difference concerns two self-consistent poles. The opposition between white and black, good and bad, sweet and bitter, does not determine the terms at stake but presupposes their existence and definition. That is why, in propositions concerning experience, negation does not ever indicate the contrary but a difference irreducible to one or more alternative predicates. When it is negated, 'is beautiful' does not give way to a new signified; rather, it undergoes an indetermination that takes it back to the negative-differential relations that are responsible for the establishment of every signified.

What we have put forward in this section can be condensed into a more general hypothesis. Logical negation benefits from the principle of the arbitrariness of the sign with regard to a given state of affairs (the fact that Socrates is just; the being sweet of a certain food, etc.). Or better: negation turns the arbitrariness of the sign into a cognitive resource or, if we prefer, into a particular operative instrument of verbal thought. I will try to explain myself in a few words. Saussure sums up his conception of arbitrariness as follows: 'Linguistic symbols have no link with what they are meant to refer to' because 'they are validated only by their reciprocal *difference*'.[14] The absence of an intrinsic relation between signs and reality is the distinctive trait of human speech. The arbitrariness of the sign implies the *non-correspondence* between words and things, propositions and facts, language and the world. It is a matter of a structural non-correspondence, caused by the negative-differential nature of language: far from obstructing it, it is precisely this non-correspondence that makes possible a fitting reference to the most disparate objects and events. Yet, we should not overlook the fact that the lack of a link between symbols in general and 'what they are meant to refer to' is in turn represented by a particular symbol: the 'not'. *Negation is the operation with which signs thematize their arbitrariness*, openly exhibiting the non-correspondence between language and the world. When it intervenes in an individual proposition, the 'not' transforms the *structural* non-correspondence, of which it is the symbolic concretion, into a *factual* non-correspondence: it is this food that does not correspond to the property of being sweet; it is Socrates who does not have any relation to the predicate 'just'. The arbitrariness of the sign, which is a basic characteristic of language, becomes in this way—through logical negation—something that the speaker invokes to correct his account of an experience or modify his way of acting.

---

14 Ibid., p. 153.

2.6
NEGATION AS LINGUISTIC CURRENCY

It is well known that Saussure was inspired—not only terminologically—by political economy, in particular, by the neoclassical theories of Walras and Pareto. The most visible trace of this inspiration is the idea that signs have a *value*, just like commodities that are bought or sold. The analogy between signs and commodities, which Saussure hints at in his lectures, remains, however, incomplete. In fact, while the economic value of a chair, a computer or a piece of clothing find a common expression in money, the linguistic values 'grass', 'red', 'love' seem instead to be devoid of a unitary representation. Yet this is only an appearance. I believe that the analogy in question can be completed without forcing it. If what I have been claiming so far on the genesis and functioning of the sign 'not' is meaningful, the following economic-linguistic definition should also be plausible: *negation is the money of language*.

Money has a twofold aspect. On the one hand, it is a commodity like all others, the circumscribed outcome of a specific work process; on the other, it reflects in itself an essential characteristic of all commodities, namely, that they have an exchange value. Of such a value, money is both the symbol and the unity of measure. The commensurability of different products of work comes together in that particular product that is money. To clarify: it is as if the Platonic idea of 'horseness' managed to acquire its own empirical existence alongside individual horses in the flesh. Just like money, linguistic negation itself has a twofold face. The 'not' is a sign among others, which does not have any sort of prestige; however, its function amounts to isolating and exhibiting a characteristic shared by all signs: the fact that each of them has a value only because it is *not* all the others. Like 'red' or 'dog', the term 'not' is determined by a set of negative relations; and yet the 'not' quintessentially expresses the negativity of the relations that determine, in general, every element of language. Money is the commodity that accounts for the value of commodities; the 'not' is the sign that accounts for the value of signs. In both cases, a part functions as an image of the whole. Both money and negation reveal the hidden nature of the system of which they are mere components.

Negation is the money of language. This definition recapitulates in shorthand the ground we have covered so far. Now, having reached the end of our itinerary and availing ourselves of this summary definition, we need to take sides with respect to the two crucial questions that have been given so much importance in philosophical reflections on negation. I mentioned them right at the beginning of this chapter, postulating that an analysis of the sign 'not' starting from the Saussurean conception of language would have allowed their radical reformulation. You will recall that the first question concerns the relation between non-being and language; the second is about the possible meta-linguistic role of negation.

Let us start with the alternative that every attempt at thinking non-being seems to be condemned to. Either non-being has its own reality independently of language, and then manifests itself within language thanks to nega-tion; or, on the contrary, non-being emerges in the expe-rience of the human animal only because it is said by the 'not', and thus as an effect or refraction of a specific linguistic operation. Both poles of this either-or have had their supporters. For example, Heidegger believes that the 'not' is limited to registering and evidencing the Nothing, preceding every enunciation, which we sense in the feeling of anxiety. 'What testifies to the constant and widespread though distorted revelation of the nothing in our existence more compellingly than negation?'[15]

Negation would be an echo that instructs us about non-being, yet only an echo, that is, the indirect attestation of an emotional mood that does not depend in any way on our words. Let us then ask what happens to the traditional either-or when we test it from Saussure's point of view. It is easy to realize that it vanishes at once. Neither of the two opposed options seems defensible any longer. If we intend to avoid the mistake denounced by Kant—namely, considering as nothing phenomena that are endowed with a positive consistency of their own, such as repulsion, displeasure, error—it is wrong to postulate a non-being that is split from language. But it is equally wrong to believe that non-being is introduced in the world by the word 'not'; precisely insofar as it is the money of language, negation only manifests in a condensed way an aspect that is already present in all verbal signs.

The 'Saussurean' solution to the age-old philosophical dilemma is roughly speaking the following: *being neither autonomous from our faculty of enunciation, nor resulting from a particular kind of statement, non-being coincides instead with the very life of language*. Non-being is indiscernible from the

---

15 Martin Heidegger, 'What Is Metaphysics?' in William McNeill (ed.), *Pathmarks* (Cambridge: Cambridge University Press, 1998[1929]), pp. 82–96; here, p. 92.

differences without positive terms that constitute this life. The nothing is therefore rooted in the very fact that we speak, and not in what we say at a given moment. It does not rise from the negative or false assertions that we happen to utter, but underlies every kind of utterance. Just as money represents the value of commodities, so the 'not' expresses the non-being of language: it expresses it but does not institute it. In a certain sense, Heidegger is right when he writes that negation testifies to 'the constant and widespread though distorted revelation of the nothing in our existence'. Yet, this nothing does not dwell in the feeling of anxiety, but in the experience of language (on Heidegger, see 4.6).

As we know, the second philosophical question revolves round the hierarchical relation between affirmation and negation. Here too discussions seem to be trapped in an unyielding either-or. For some, the 'not' is an integral part of the object-language, since it plays a considerable role in the assertions that describe events and states of affairs. Austin writes: 'Affirmation and negation are exactly on a level, in this sense, that no language can exist which does not contain conventions for both and that both refer to the world equally directly, not to statements about the world.'[16]

For other authors, the 'not' performs a clear meta-linguistic function, since it refers (at least implicitly) to a previous statement. Russell writes: 'The word "not" is only significant when attached to a sentence, and therefore presupposes language. Consequently, if "p" is a sentence of the

---

16 John Langshaw Austin, 'Truth' in *Philosophical Papers* (Oxford: Oxford University Press, 1979[1950]), pp. 128–9.

primary language, "not-*p*" is a sentence of the secondary language.'[17]

Faced with such an open contrast, we should ask: Is it really necessary to privilege one of the two options? What we have said so far about the sign 'not' and its genesis from the primary negativity of language suggests an answer: neither one nor the other.

Negation is certainly asymmetrical with respect to affirmation, since it deals with the relation between propositions and facts, without enhancing or modifying at all the representation of the facts under consideration. But the judgement of existence and the attribution of number are also asymmetrical with regard to descriptive predicates ('is green', 'is tall', etc.). Not to mention the modal clauses 'is possible' and 'is necessary', whose task— precisely like that of negation—amounts exclusively to qualifying the relation between the sentences in which they appear and the states of affairs of things in the world: Who would be prepared to ascribe them to meta-language? Against Austin, the asymmetry—that is, the actual difference of logical level—between affirmation and negation is undeniable. But, against Russell, asymmetry does not at all entail a 'secondary language'. I will try to clarify this. In ordinary communication, we never fail to use *reflexive* expressions, that is, expressions that provide information about the statement that includes them or, more generally, about the very nature of verbal activity. Passing them off as meta-linguistic tools is a symptom of inebriation. Among these expressions, disseminated across discourses of the

---

17 Bertrand Russell, *An Inquiry into Meaning and Truth* (Abingdon: Routledge, 1992[1940]), p. 64.

'primary language' (tales, disputes, prayers, etc.), the most relevant place rests with negation. What matters then is individuating the particular *reflexivity* of the sign 'not', which is obviously very different from that inherent to the attribution of a number or the modal clause 'is possible'.

We saw earlier (2.4 and 2.1) that negation is the specialized spokesperson for the 'complex of eternally negative differences' in which consists the value of each linguistic term. The formative process of phonemes, morphemes and lemmas coalesces in it. The asymmetry of the 'not' with regard to other signs is analogous to the asymmetry of the dollar or the euro vis-à-vis other commodities. Like money, negation is devoted to representing the unapparent texture of the jigsaw of which it is only a component: it is here that its specific *reflexive* performance lies. Like money, the 'not' is itself a part that reflects the whole. But the reflection of the whole (the internal organization of language) carried out by the part (negation) should not be confused with the employment of meta-language. It is in fact evident that a statement of the secondary language is far from mimetically reproducing the properties of the statement of the primary language of which it speaks, and should instead distance itself from them. The alternative between object-language and meta-language obscures, or in any case distorts, the actual role of negation, that is, transforming what language *is* into something that language *expresses*. We know that the 'not' is a *commutator*: it applies the negative-differential relations between words to the events and affects these words refer to; it enforces in a single empirical judgement the structural non-correspondence between signs and reality. Precisely insofar as it converts the way of (not) being of language into a particular communicative resource, negation is one of the main axes of human nature. Deferring the satisfaction of desire, reshaping drives, contradicting the ruling order, punctuating time as 'not any longer' and 'not yet'; all this, and many other things, would not be possible if the primary negativity of language were not embodied in an independent symbol. That is, all of this would not be possible if language did not have its money.

3.

The Meaning of 'Meaning'[1]

3.1
BEYOND SAUSSURE

It is worth spelling out again, plainly and without precautions, the theoretical hypothesis this book revolves around, at least in part. Negation crystallizes a pervasive characteristic of human discourse; it isolates and concentrates in itself a physiognomic trait of all verbal signs; it bestows an autonomous prominence on what makes a

---

1 Throughout the book, 'significato' has been rendered as 'meaning'. Saussure's 'signifié', which Virno does not translate, has been translated as 'signified'. Wherever possible 'senso' has been rendered as 'sense'; in some cases, I opted for 'meaning' for linguistic reasons. [Trans.]

word, a proposition and a language what they are. Far from extending the opposition between physical forces or the contrast between psychological drives, the syntactic connective 'not' has a *reflexive* genesis, since it refers above all to certain basic prerogatives of the system to which it belongs. If the genesis of the 'not' is reflexive, its applications are nevertheless fully extroversive; it participates in the description of the world and determines to a great extent the form assumed by the actions and passions of the human animal. These two aspects are neither incompatible nor merely coexistent but, in fact, complementary. We do not understand anything about the extroversive functioning of the 'not'—for example, the way in which it enters into the recounting of an empirical event—if we neglect its reflexive genesis. Negation exerts a cognitive and pragmatic role of great importance precisely because it condenses a ubiquitous property, which belongs to the very nature of our speaking, into a particular syntactic connective, which assists the most disparate verbal performances ('The rose is *not* red,' 'Do *not* harass me,' etc.). Going back once again to the formula we have been using as a refrain and as a central idea in our investigation, we could say that negation exerts a cognitive and pragmatic role of great importance precisely because it converts that which language *is* into something language *expresses*.

In the previous chapter, I have claimed that this theoretical hypothesis finds an indirect but robust support in Saussure's texts. According to him, language is a 'complex of eternally negative differences', that is, an organism characterized by the lack of atomic elements that subsist by themselves. The value of a phonological or lexical entity depends entirely on countless oppositions: x means something only because it is *not y*, or *z*, or *w*, etc. If this is the case, we cannot avoid recognizing that the first and decisive function of the sign 'not' amounts to a recapitulation of the process of formation of all signs. As a linguistic phenomenon among others, the 'not' unveils the general outline of the phenomena we call linguistic. Negation as a logical operation is amphibious and Janus-faced: on the one hand, it mirrors the non-being inherent to the inner life of language (x has a value only because it is *not y*, or *z*, or *w*, etc.); on the other, it transfers this non-being to discourses that concern our experience ('Luca is *not* vindictive'). However powerful and instructive it might be, Saussure's position is not binding. My theoretical hypothesis stands or falls short independently of it. Those who fully agree with Saussure's *Course in General Linguistics* could reject my hypothesis without hesitation; just as, conversely, we cannot rule out the possibility that it may be embraced by those who, judging Saussurean structuralism to be abstruse and dated, identify in Chomsky's generative grammar the authentic focal point of modern linguistics. What really matters—I repeat—is the link between an original negativity, which characterizes the very existence of our language, and negation strictly speaking, which operates only in some statements. Saussure offered us a good opportunity to take a look at such link. But it was nothing more than an opportunity: his conception of language as a set of 'differences without positive terms' is a particular version—suggestive but not exhaustive—of that original negativity from which, in my opinion, the connective 'not' arises. Other versions should be inventoried and discussed. To confirm the idea that negation is the money of language, we now need to introduce new arguments and invoke new authors who are very far from Saussure.

In the pages that follow, the focus will be on the gap that separates the sense [*senso*] of a statement from a psychological representation. Over the last decades, this gap—on which Frege insisted—has been repudiated and even laughed at by the cognitive sciences, according to which both the laws of logic and the dynamics of social systems need to be fully brought back, piece by piece, to psychology. By repudiating such a careless repudiation, I would like to show that a linguistic meaning [*significato*] really diverges from any kind of mental picture (so, with regard to Frege, we should declare: not everything he says is right, but he is almost never wrong). But I would also like to show that, contrary to Frege, such a divergence depends only on negation. It is the prerequisites of the sign 'not' that make it possible for verbal meanings to have an impersonal nature which is radically public and irreducible to the operations carried out by individual minds. We should therefore not be surprised that the ancient and modern proponents of the primacy of psychology have repeatedly wagered on the possibility of providing a psychologistic interpretation of negation (and, in particular, of its genesis). But we should be even less surprised that, having lost their specific wager, they are now stripped of resources and on the edge of complete bankruptcy.

3.2

NEGATION AND MENTAL PICTURES

There is nothing in a psychological representation that enables us to distinguish it from the fact it represents. The mental picture, as picture, is not able to trace a border between itself and its object. The state of affairs that I perceive, remember or prefigure does not enjoy any autonomy with respect to the corresponding perceptive, mnemonic or prefigurative act, and amounts instead to an inner articulation of this same act. Since it only accounts for what itself puts forward ('to put forward' is indeed the literal meaning of the German verb *vorstellen*, 'to represent'), representation never relates to something heterogeneous which may transcend it: the success I hope for does not have any physiognomy other than the one it draws from the hope for success; the Mont Blanc I depict is one thing with my depiction of the Mont Blanc. One would be tempted to say that the meaning of a mental picture invariably coincides with its reference; or, in the end, that the sign is also the thing it stands for. But 'meaning' and 'reference' are misleading terms, since what is at stake here is a cognitive activity that is not linguistic. For the time being, let us limit ourselves to establishing that the existence of representation is as such a guarantee for the reality of what is represented. On a philosophical level, the equivalence between psychic operations and facts has taken the bizarre and extravagant shape of a doubt about the existence of the external world. But, on close inspection, what is bizarre and extravagant is not so much this doubt but, rather, its implicit—and apparently more respectable—presupposition: namely, the primacy, or worse the monopoly, that would pertain to psychological representation, that is, *Vorstellung*, in the experience of the human animal.

The source of the situation we have just described is not, let it be clear, the time of early infancy, in which every psychic drive has the consistency of a real event and every real event resembles a psychic drive.[2] Given that in early infancy a sort of symbiotic unity between mind and world prevails, no phenomenon can really be said to be interior or exterior. With regard to this ontogenetic stage, it would be wrong to speak of a coincidence between representations and facts, given that there is not yet any 'representation' or 'fact'. The polarity between representation and fact emerges only later, at the time when a caesura between psyche and environment, self and non-self, interiority and exteriority has been affirmed. The crucial point is that, even if it specifically emerges from it, the polarity between representation and fact is not able to conform to the caesura and, instead, betrays it again and again. The peculiar trait of this polarity is the revocation of the very distinction that made it possible. The indiscernibility between perception and the perceived object, hope and the event one hopes for, memory and the remembered circumstance is worthy of our attention precisely because it stands out against the background of the achieved division between mind and world. The psychic subject notices that his representation is not identical with the represented fact, but, to the extent that he represents and until he limits himself to representing, he does not find a way to express this non-identity.

---

2 See Sigmund Freud, 'Fetishism' in James Strachey (ed.), *The Standard Edition of the Complete Psychological Works of Sigmund Freud, Volume 21* (London: Vintage, 2001[1927]), pp. 149–57. See also Massimo De Carolis, *Il paradosso antropologico. Nicchie, micromondi e dissociazione psichica* (Macerata: Quodlibet, 2008).

The permanent discrepancy between mental pictures and states of affairs, which mostly remains hidden, manifests itself at times by means of revocations and disappointments: and yet there is no mental picture able to document these occasional impasses, or, even less, the permanent discrepancy of which they are the warning sign. I psychologically represent two friends, Andrea and Giovanni, who are fencing. I envision them with all the pertinent perceptual details: the protective masks, the sound of the foils, the furniture of the gym, Giovanni's impetuous attack, Andrea's awkward defence, etc. A little later, however, I recall that precisely on that day the two decided not to train as usual. I am then led to rectify the mental picture I elaborated in the first instance, which is no doubt illusory. It is here that the *Vorstellung*, the psychological representation, stumbles upon its characteristic limit. I cannot depict an Andrea and Giovanni who, quite simply, are not fencing. A picture never shows how things are not. To account for the training they skipped, I will represent my friends as busy with activities that are completely different from fencing. I now envision them taking a walk, or reading the newspaper or flirting with a woman. But none of these supplementary pictures, all of which refer to new events that are positive, exhibits the fallacy of the original picture; none of them is able to refute it, bringing into focus the mistake it succumbed to. The revocation of a *Vorstellung* is never transformed into the *Vorstellung* of a revocation.

The impossibility of producing a negative representation, whose only task would be to show the inadequacy of a previous representation, is the direct consequence or corollary of a far more radical impossibility: that of distinguishing representation in general—whether impeccable or fallacious—from the represented fact. The picture of Andrea and Giovanni fencing cannot be refuted, but only replaced, because—like any other picture—it does not keep any distance from its object, appearing at the same time as a sign and a designated thing. To put it the other way round: the *contingent* gap between an illusory representation and reality would be representable in turn if, and only if, it were possible to represent the *persistent* gap dividing each representation, even the most faithful and perspicuous, from what it puts forward. But the *Vorstellung* does not have any means to express this second and more fundamental gap. What ratifies that the mental picture of my cat sitting on the armchair does not equate with the fact that my cat is sitting on the armchair is an apparatus that falls outside mental pictures: linguistic negation.

In a note of 26 November 1914, Wittgenstein writes: 'So, can one negate a picture? No. And in this lies the difference between picture and proposition.'[3] Negation is the ridge that separates verbal thought from psychological representation. All further differences that we happen to observe when we confront a statement or a *Vorstellung* derive from this ridge, or merge with it. But there is more: in addition to instituting a neat discontinuity between the linguistic and psychological fields, negation is the privileged means through which the former is grafted onto the latter, reorganizing it extensively. The cognitive value of

---

3 Ludwig Wittgenstein, *Notebooks, 1914–1916* (Oxford: Blackwell, 1961), p. 33.

mental pictures is partially modified by the very 'not' that conversely determines the fracture between mental pictures and propositions. Note that what is now at stake is not the status of negative statements but only the *retroaction* of the 'not' on psychological representations. This retroaction is always operative once we learn to speak and, in particular, to say how things are *not*, since it is certain that we never stop producing psychological representations which as such are indistinguishable from the facts they put forward. What I really want to stress is the role fulfilled by negation in determining a *phase of transition* between mental pictures and discourses. In the passage of which I earlier quoted only the beginning, Wittgenstein offers a synthetic account of this phase of transition, during which the picture is no longer what it used to be and discourse still includes a non-verbal component. Let us quote it in full: 'So, can one negate a picture? No. And in this lies the difference between picture and proposition. The picture can serve as a proposition. But in that case something gets added to it which brings it about that now it *says* something. In short: I can only deny that the picture is right, but the *picture* I cannot deny.'[4]

What follows is an indirect commentary on these elliptical observations made by Wittgenstein. It is worth asking what is the element that, being added to the picture, makes it '*say* something'.

The statement 'Mont Blanc is thus and so' can always take the place of the mental picture I formed of Mont Blanc. However, in this case, verbal language is not grafted onto a psychological representation but weakens it; it does

---

4 Ibid.

not modify its prerogatives but leaves them behind as a by-now irrelevant residue. For discourse to retroact on the *Vorstellung* it is necessary that the two terms not elide each other but that they be present simultaneously and relate to one other. One could at this stage ask: What does this retroaction based on coexistence amount to? There is an episode in modern art that can help us answer this question, as it offers a theoretical model of general value: the inscription *ceci n'est pas une pipe* that Magritte included in his painting of a pipe. The negative statement 'this is not a pipe' is part of the picture of which it speaks: it does not put it aside or replace it but integrates it. More precisely, the negative statement brings to light an essential characteristic of the picture which it can never express as picture: its *not* being what it shows. If I have mentioned Magritte's eloquent painting, it was only to get straight to the point. And the point is that the articulation between language and *Vorstellungen* fully relies on a negation: 'Representation is *not* the fact it represents.' Without intervening in any way in the specific content of a given *Vorstellung*, the 'not' limits itself to evidencing the persistent gap that subsists between any *Vorstellung* and the object it depicts. Accompanying like a *basso continuo* all psychological representations (even the most fitting), negation to a certain extent changes their functioning. As soon as it is subjected to the *ceci n'est pas* . . . representation no longer coincides with the represented fact but stands for it, that is, *designates* it. When the 'not' grants it that distance from reality that is typical of signs, the picture is inserted into a network of verbal meanings and, in Wittgenstein's words, can even 'serve as a proposition'. Negation is therefore the element that, being added to the picture from the outside, makes it '*say* something'.

First, negation makes apparent the *persistent* gap between representations and facts: the picture of the pipe is *not* ever a pipe. But it is precisely the expression of this permanent gap that enables us also to exhibit the *contingent* gap between an individual representation that is fallacious and the actual course of the world. The revocation of an erroneous picture is made possible only if the 'not' has already sanctioned that no picture, however correct it might be, is identical with the corresponding state of affairs. We need now to pay attention to the way in which negation operates when an inadequate or illusory *Vorstellung* is at stake. Let us return to the example discussed earlier: I depict Andrea and Giovanni as they fence, but shortly thereafter I realize they are not fencing. How can we account for this *occasional* impasse of the representational activity with the help of a syntactic connective, the 'not', whose main function in the psychological domain is to signal the *permanent* heterogeneity of representation with respect to represented facts?

It would be grossly mistaken to claim that the statement 'Andrea and Giovanni are *not* fencing' carries out a refutation of the fallacious picture. It is of course true that this statement shows the typical power of linguistic negation: the one who utters it is still speaking of Andrea and Giovanni fencing, and not of the other activities the two friends are engaging in; moreover, while this person speaks of it, or indeed because he speaks of it, he excludes it. But acknowledging that language, unlike pictures, is able to indicate what is *not* happening, is not of great help if we want to understand in what way language tackles a particular picture and, without liquidating or replacing it, denounces its vacuity. The statement 'Andrea and Giovanni are *not* fencing' has no point of contact with psychological representations. It thus does not oppose my picture of the two fencers but only the contradictory statement 'Andrea and Giovanni are fencing.' This should be enough to deal with the gross mistake. The entire difficulty lies in recognizing that the illusory picture which we wish to refute is and remains undeniable. When I presume to negate it, I am no longer dealing with the picture but with one of its linguistic doubles. It is possible to really refute a picture, and avoid tacitly equating it with an assertion, but only on condition of safeguarding the fact that it is undeniable. Concretely, how does a refutation that respects such a provision proceed? What belies a deceiving *Vorstellung* is indeed a negative statement, but this is a negative statement at a logical level higher than that of the object-language. Without saying anything about the fact represented by the *Vorstellung*, it dwells exclusively on the latter's properties. Let us consider a judgement of the kind: 'The picture of Andrea and Giovanni fencing is *not* correct.' Rather than being applied to the state of affairs that the erroneous picture puts forward (as happened in the first-level descriptive statement 'Andrea and Giovanni are *not* fencing'), the 'not' here aims at the very validity of a picture that has no corresponding state of affairs. It seems that this is precisely the solution adumbrated by Wittgenstein: 'I can only deny that the picture is right, but the *picture* I cannot deny.' Language establishes a direct relation with a psychological representation (which is as such undeniable) only if, refraining from describing the fragment of the world that the representation puts forward, it limits itself to formulating a reflexive judgement on the outcome of the cognitive activity. That is, only if it gives up on dealing with the object around which the representation revolves in order to treat the representation itself as an object.

To sum up, the 'not' intervenes in the realm of *Vorstellungen* in two different ways. On the one hand, it expresses a trait shared by all mental pictures: 'The picture is *not* what it shows.' On the other, it documents the failure ascribable to an individual picture: 'This picture is *not* true.' In the first case, negation has an *ontological* dimension, since it provides us with information about the way of being of psychological representations, revealing their structural non-identity with the states of affairs they depict. In the second, negation instead has an *empirical* dimension, given that it registers the occasional discordance between a faulty representation and the reality of facts. In sanctioning that 'the picture is *not* what it shows,' ontological negation explicitly relates the *Vorstellung* to the caesura between mind and world, self and non-self, interiority and exteriority, which it both presupposes and obscures. Empirical negation, which is responsible for the judgement 'This picture is *not* true,' makes it possible for revocation and the *Vorstellung* to intersect and penetrate each other, rather than remaining two independent phenomena, doomed at most to alternating with each other. Let me now add a remark which should be taken as a warning: if the 'not' carries out a twofold—ontological and empirical—function when it retroacts as an alien body on psychological representations, it is only because it already carries out this twofold function in its natural habitat, that is, in language. In addition to appearing in statements that speak openly of what does not happen (empirical function), negation especially exhibits something that pertains to the way of being of all statements, including obviously affirmative ones (ontological function). In the following pages, we will have to discuss this crucial issue at length.

3.3
FRACTURES INTERNAL TO THE STATEMENT

Mental pictures are not identical with the states of affairs they show: this is what no picture is able to show. The disjuncture between psychological representations and facts can never itself be represented. It is only the sign 'not' that expresses such a disjuncture. But although it illustrates an essential aspect of psychological representation, the 'not' has nothing in common with the latter. Negation is an exclusive prerogative of verbal thought. Consequently, expressing the disjuncture between representations and facts by means of the 'not' is a step that leads us *beyond the field of representations*. Or better: it is a step that institutes the most original and incontrovertible watershed between verbal thought and representations, speech and perception, logic and psychology.

It is easy to recognize the independence of verbal thought from *Vorstellungen*: a discourse on jealousy or on the war in Iraq can be uttered and understood without resorting to mental pictures; in fact, it is what it is—that is, a discourse—precisely because it exempts both the speaker and the listener from *placing before themselves*[5] the emotion or event in question. It is less easy, but more interesting, to grasp the point of rupture between the two

5 Virno is here evoking the literal sense of *Vorstellung*. [Trans.]

planes. This point—which is untraceable if we are happy to repeat as a mantra that statements diverge in many regards from representations—is instead unveiled in the way in which a specific component of statements, the 'not', intervenes on representations from the outside. The point of rupture is also a tangential point. Language irrevocably separates itself from the *Vorstellung* when it repudiates its claims and introduces in its regard a distinction (the *Vorstellung* of *y* is something different from *y*) that is precluded to the *Vorstellung*. Verifying the gap between pictures and reality means verifying at the same time the gap between words and pictures. In the form of an inference: *If* (I ascertain that) representation is not the represented fact, *then* (I also ascertain that) a statement is not a representation. The pure and simple formulation of the premise is sufficient, in this case, to prove the veracity of the conclusion; the first disjunction, 'representation is *not* the represented fact,' is the performative demonstration of the second, 'a statement is *not* a representation.'

> *Note: The Constitutional Principle of the 'Third Realm'.*
> It is well known that Frege was committed to tracing a neat division between *Vorstellungen* and the sense of statements (a sense which he also calls 'thought'). The former need a 'bearer', that is, they entirely depend on the activities and vicissitudes of an individual mind; the latter is public, shared by everybody and owned by nobody—'without a bearer'—and as objective as the moon or an earthquake. If the sense of statements did not differ from *Vorstellungen*, we would not have any foothold for distinguishing *Vorstellungen* from the facts they depict. Frege believes that the erroneous reduction of linguistic meanings to a jumble of

psychological representations makes doubting the existence of an external world not only legitimate but also inevitable. Those who support such a reduction prove Berkeley right: 'Their *esse* [of things] is *percipi*, nor is it possible they should have any existence, out of the minds or thinking things which perceive them.'[6] There is no third way: 'Either the thesis that only what is in my representation can be the object of my awareness is false, or all my knowledge and perception is restricted to the range of my representations, to the stage of my self-consciousness. In this case, I should have only an inner world.'[7] What guarantees the separation between representations and facts, and thus also the reality of a world that does not coincide with psychic activity, is something that deviates from both representations and facts: the set of linguistic meanings, that is, the verbal thought that Frege magniloquently names 'third realm'.

The sensible world becomes an *external* world—autonomous from the *Vorstellungen* inherent to this or that 'bearer'—when it is *said*. As impersonal as the rain that drenches everyone equally, language inserts spatiotemporal phenomena into a public dimension, enabling their common experience (provided that we understand 'common' as what overcomes from the start the mental pictures of individuals, not their weighted average). Linguistic meanings, which are not at all perceptible, nonetheless constitute an essential

---

6 George Berkeley, *Philosophical Works* (London: Everyman, 1975[1710]), p. 90.

7 Gottlob Frege, 'Thought: A Logical Inquiry' in B. McGuiness (ed.), *Collected Papers in Mathematics, Logic, and Philosophy* (Oxford: Blackwell, 1984[1918–19]), pp. 351–72; here, p. 364.

element of the most immediate perception: 'Having visual impressions is, indeed, necessary for *seeing things*, but it is not sufficient. What has still to be added is not anything sensible. And yet it is precisely this which opens up the external world for us; for without this non-sensible component each person would remain shut up within his own inner world.'[8] I can *see* a stormy sea as an object independent from my consciousness thanks to the 'non-sensible component' that is the proposition 'the sea is stormy.' The violence of the waves, if described by a proposition, distances itself from psychological representations and rises to the level of an event of the external world. But there is a crucial point, which Frege overlooks, or at least does not make explicit: the proposition 'the sea is stormy' has an impersonal meaning, which can be understood also by those who do not have any representation of the violence of the waves, because it can be converted at any time into 'the sea is *not* stormy.' While being actual only in some cases, negation is always and in any case at work as a potential negation. The public character of linguistic meanings is one with the permanent possibility of their *deniability*. The absence of a 'bearer' goes together with the constant threat of the 'not'. Deniability, without which both the sense and the comprehension of statements would dissolve, attests to the fact that the states of affairs of which we speak subsist (or do not subsist) outside of our minds. It is not simply the world we speak about that is external but also the world about which we can negate everything we say.

The 'third realm' is inhabited by statements that have a public sense—as such independent of individual

---

8 Ibid., p. 369 (emphasis added).

psychic processes—precisely because they are deniable. The 'third realm' is coextensive with the field in which the 'not' functions (it does not really matter whether actually or potentially). But the 'not' manifests its effects even when material things of the external world are not at stake. Verbal thought includes countless statements that, although subject to negation and *hence* 'without a bearer', do not, however, have any spatiotemporal equivalent: '5 is a prime number,' 'God is omnipotent,' etc. Frege's passage continues as follows: 'So perhaps, since the decisive factor lies in the non-sensible, something non-sensible, even without the cooperation of sense impressions, could [. . .] enable us to grasp thoughts.'[9] The 'third realm' defends the rights of the external world, and yet it overcomes it, distancing itself from it. More precisely, it overcomes it and distances itself from it by virtue of the deniability/public character of the linguistic meanings that allowed it to defend the rights of the external world. 'The non-sensible component' that, according to Frege, ensures a shared meaning both to the proposition about the violence of the waves and to the one about prime numbers or God is ascribable, in the first and last instance, to the syntactic connective 'not'.

The first two realms postulated by Frege—mental pictures and physical reality—could not remain two, but would blend and become indiscernible, if the realm of deniable statements were not added to them. It is like saying: either one or three, but never just two. The three realms are analogous to the vertices of a triangle: they stand apart and yet are correlated; or better, they are correlated insofar as they stand apart.

---

9 Ibid.

The sides of the triangle, in which is condensed the distance that separates each vertex from the others, amount to three negative assertions of basic importance: (1) representations are *not* the external world; (2) verbal thought is *not* a representation; (3) verbal thought is *not* the external world. Here, the asymmetry I have already mentioned stands out: it is exclusively verbal thought, that is, *one* of the separated vertices of the triangle, that determines the separation between *all* the vertices and thus enables the existence of the triangle. As the constitutional principle of the 'third realm', negation also qualifies in turn the relations between the 'third realm' and the other two, as well as that between the first (psychological representations) and the second (spatiotemporal facts).

As I was saying, negation is an exclusive prerogative of verbal thought. It does not have any precursor in sensible experience or in emotional turmoil: unless, of course, we wish to consider vomiting or flight as an incipient form of negative proposition. Confusing the *retroaction* of the 'not' on perceptions and affects with a perceptive or affective *genesis* of the 'not' is an extraordinary error. It is quite similar to understanding the industrial transformation of alpine valleys as a naturalistic, or better, geological, omen of the industry of the future. While being a particular region of verbal thought, negation offers a topographical map of the totality of the territory in which it is comprised. According to Auroux, 'Language is a system regulated by the image of itself.'[10] I

10 Sylvain Auroux, *La révolution technologique de la grammatisation. Introduction à l'histoire des sciences du langage* (Liège: Mardaga, 1994), p. 16.

share this view, but I would also add: what provides this regulatory self-portrait is precisely and only the 'not'. Everything depends on understanding of which salient aspects of human speech or, more precisely, of which of its internal divisions, is negation, at the same time, the repercussion and the diagram.

A first remark, rudimentary yet unavoidable: while the distinction between psychological representations and facts cannot ever be *represented*, the distinction between statements and facts can always be *enunciated* thanks to the 'not' which is an intrinsic element of enunciation. Although it mostly remains tacit, the acknowledgment that 'the statement is *not* the fact of which it speaks' constitutes the background and the presupposition of every verbal utterance. Our discourses, unlike mental pictures, contain in themselves the index of their non-coincidence with reality. This index consists of the same syntactic connective that also sanctions, but only externally, the fracture between pictures and states of affairs. In order to stress the difference between the two cases, it is worth introducing a terminological variation: the 'not' *signals* the non-identity between representations and facts; yet it *reflects* the non-identity between statements and facts. I say 'reflects' because, in the second case, negation evidences a fundamental characteristic of the field to which it belongs.

But is this kind of approach reliable? Not entirely, as always happens with shorthand abbreviations of very articulated structures. Its great flaw lies in preserving an unaltered notion of 'fact' even when a discourse is at stake. It seems to me that this notion is strongly linked to psychological representation. The 'fact' is the other face of the *Vorstellung*, its inseparable Siamese twin. The two terms—both extra-linguistic—hold or fall apart together. It is therefore at the very least inaccurate to claim that the 'not', in addition to *signalling* the fracture between representations and facts, *reflects* that between statements and facts. A statement never limits itself to replacing a representation, so as to then concern itself with a fact; rather, it introjects the entire polarity between representation and fact, radically transforming it. Let us see how this takes place. As Frege writes, 'A fact is a statement that is true.'[11] And the being true (or false) of a statement is an integrally linguistic property, entwined but not identical with that other, equally linguistic, property that is the statement's formulation of a thought. The psychological polarity between representation and fact gives way to the logical polarity between semantic content and truth-value, whose extremes are located within the same speech act. The two elements that compose the new couple are heterogeneous, autonomous, and at times even divergent: the thought formulated by a statement, that is, its *sense*, cannot be assimilated to the truth of the statement, that is, its *denotation*. Negation does not directly designate the gap between language and reality but a split inherent to language itself: sense is *not* denotation. The word 'not' *reflects* this split that is present in all words. Reflected and condensed in a specific sign, the split between sense and denotation becomes an independent logical operator that can be applied to the most diverse linguistic games. If you

11 Frege, 'Thought: A Logical Inquiry', p. 368. This is usually rendered in English as 'A fact is a thought [*Gedanke*] that is true.' [Trans.]

were then to ask me whether, in the end, it is really incorrect to say that 'a statement is *not* the fact of which we speak,' I would reply: obviously not, as long as it is perfectly clear that the discrepancy thus evidenced between discourses and states of affairs is only the overt symptom, or the weakened echo, of a discrepancy (or, in Platonic jargon, a *diaíresis*, division) already present in our discourses.

The mere possibility of stating that 'the grass is *not* green' guarantees that the sense of 'the grass is green' does not coincide with its denotation; or, more roughly, that 'the grass is green' is not a green grass. *The sign 'not' expresses the difference between sense and denotation*, which—and this is crucial—is a characteristic shared by any descriptive locution. But, in expressing it, the 'not' turns the general difference between sense and denotation into a specific component of the sense of some statements: 'The grass is *not* green,' 'Michele does *not* fancy Marina,' etc. Statements are negative when their semantic content comprises the sign that attests the non-identity between semantic content and reference. Previously, when we examined the various ways in which the 'not' retroacts on psychological representations, we observed that the 'not' has both an ontological function ('representation is *not* ever the represented fact') and an empirical one ('the representation of Andrea and Giovanni fencing is *not* correct'). However, already at that stage, we assumed that the 'not' exerts this twofold function in the field of *Vorstellungen*—where it works as an intruder—only because it first exerts it within verbal thought—where it actually dwells. This point can now easily be grasped. I call primary, but also ontological, that negation which mirrors a peculiar trait or, better, a peculiar fracture of human language considered as a whole: 'Sense is *not* ever denotation.' I call secondary, but also empirical or contingent, that negation which evidences, already in the meaning of a particular statement, the lack of denotation by which that statement is affected: 'Luigi does *not* live in the United States.'

It is reasonable to say that the 'not' designates the difference between sense and denotation, but it is also insufficient. This diagnosis does not explain the nature and role of negation in pragmatic statements (orders, prayers, promises, admonitions, etc.), which are always devoid of a denotation, that is, of a truth-value. What happens with sentences charged with emotions such as 'I beg you *not* to go away' or 'I am *not* begging you to stay with me'? I am of the view that the syntactic connective 'not' reflects and condenses in itself a second division internal to our discourses, which is very different from that between sense and denotation; different but no less fundamental and, perhaps, even more pervasive. In order to identify it, it is necessary to take a step back, paying attention to an aspect of psychological representation that we have ignored so far.

As it is indistinguishable from the fact it itself puts forward, representation is also indistinguishable from the *emotional stimulus* that causes it. Desire, repulsion, fear, hope, emulation, diffidence, aggressiveness, uncertainty; these are some of the relevant names of the drive with which the *Vorstellung* coincides at a given moment. I would like to make three quick remarks. First, to the extent that they are both inseparable from representation, the psychic drive and the depicted state of affairs turn out to be correlated, even equivalent. In the *Vorstellung*, the drive is already a state of affairs and the state of affairs is still a drive. Moreover, given that it joins the emotional stimulus, the mental picture is never reducible to a disinterested cognitive operation but, rather, has the nature of an operative behaviour. The picture is as such the trigger or the instrument of an action. Finally, the strong identity between representation and stimulus excludes the possibility of representing the inhibition of the stimulus. The only way in which the blocking of an imaginative drive (say, about sex) can be manifested is in its replacement with a new imaginative drive (say, about food or a cross-country race).

Verbal thought subverts these relations, disjoining what is inbuilt and even inextricable in the *Vorstellung*. A statement is independent from the psychological stimulus that both precedes and accompanies it. But the notion of 'stimulus', like the notion of 'fact', befits representations, not discourses. Hence, claiming that the statement does *not* coincide with the emotional stimulus is only an approximate version of the important point at stake here. The couple representation/stimulus, just like the couple representation/fact, is included as a whole within the statement, where it undergoes a drastic metamorphosis. Returning to an observation made by Frege,[12] Austin[13] speaks of 'illocutionary force' to indicate the *action* we carry out when we say something: asserting, ordering, exhorting,

---

12 See Gottlob Frege, 'Sense and Reference' (1892), *The Philosophical Review* 57(3) (May 1948): 209–30.

13 John Langshaw Austin, *How to Do Things with Words* (Oxford: Oxford University Press, 1962).

wishing somebody luck, taking an oath, cursing. The 'illocutionary force' is the verbal correspondent of the psychological stimulus. Frege and Austin carefully distinguish sense from statement, for example, Mario's generosity from the various linguistic acts in which it may appear: the question 'Is Mario generous?'; the true or false assertion 'Mario is generous;' the plea 'Mario, be generous,' etc. The non-identity between statements and stimulus is unveiled as the non-identity between two components of the same statement: sense is *not* the illocutionary force. When the truth-value of our words is at stake, that is, only in assertions, negation expresses the gap between sense and denotation, or, roughly speaking, between statements and facts; when, on the other hand, speech as action is at stake, that is, in all discourses (including of course assertions), negation expresses the gap between sense and illocutionary force, or, roughly speaking, between statements and emotional stimuli.

The permanent difference between sense and illocutionary force, of which the 'not' is the symbol (ontological negation), becomes at times explicit within an individual statement (empirical negation). More precisely, it becomes explicit in two different ways, each of which concurs in defining the typically human form of the adaptive resource that is inhibition.

(a) I call *internal* the empirical negation that appears in statements such as 'I order you *not* to go to Rome,' 'We swear we do *not* remember the torments of civil war,' 'I wish you would *not* meet the police.' This negation leaves the illocutionary force intact (the ordering, swearing, wishing), yet it annuls the event or conduct that the sense continues to propose (going to Rome; remembering the torments; meeting the police). The action we carry out by speaking remains unvaried but the semantic content is turned upside down; the persistent non-identity between these two aspects of our sentences is thus revealed. While the emotional stimulus on which the *Vorstellung* hinges perfectly corresponds to the represented fact, the illocutionary force can always be resolved into the interdiction of the state of affairs it is invoking. If they are followed by the 'not', the verbs (to order, to swear, etc.) in which the illocutionary force is embodied set up a paradoxical stimulus to abstain, renounce, omit, which is inconceivable in the realm of mental pictures. Internal negation concerns only pragmatic statements, not assertions; in 'I assert that the sea is *not* stormy,' the 'not' only registers the split between sense and denotation, and certainly not the gap between illocutionary force (the act of asserting) and sense (the being stormy of the sea).

(b) On the other hand, I call *external* the empirical negation at work in statements like 'I do *not* promise I will be faithful to you,' 'I do *not* plead the court for clemency,' 'I do *not* encourage you to fight in Afghanistan.' This negation does not touch the semantic content of the promise, plea or encouragement but dissolves the very linguistic act of promising, pleading and encouraging. Sense remains unvaried, and the illocutionary force is deactivated: that is how, in this case, the independence of the former from the latter emerges. While the indiscernibility of representation and psychic drive prevents us from representing the blocking of the drive, the heterogeneity between sense and illocutionary force always allows us to enunciate the blocking of the illocutionary force. External negation also involves assertions; in saying 'I do *not* assert that the sea is stormy,' we evidence the paralysis of the act of asserting, not the lack of a denotation.

In both (a) and (b) negation works like an inhibitory brake. But if in (a) the 'not' contributes to the formation of an *inhibiting stimulus*, in (b) it instead determines the *inhibition of the stimulus* as such. To inhibit means only to suspend without substituting. Internal negation ('I order you *not* to go to Rome') bans a certain conduct but does not indicate an alternative. External negation ('I do *not* encourage you to . . .', 'I do *not* assert that . . .') sabotages the illocutionary force which is nonetheless mentioned but does not specify which other illocutionary force takes its place. In this inclination to *suspend without substituting*, made possible only by the logical operator 'not', we should recognize a characteristic trait of human praxis, or even an anthropogenetic apparatus.

Negation is a circumscribed aspect of linguistic activity, which, however, illustrates the way of being of verbal language in its totality. It provides a clear X-ray of the biological organ of which it is a part. The primary function of the 'not' in fact amounts to designating the two *diairéseis*, or 'divisions' which, in addition to being present in each statement, also define what a statement is in general: sense is *not* denotation; sense is *not* the illocutionary force. These two caesurae should be understood as partial articulations of a far more radical fracture: *sense is not something present*. Let me explain this point. The texture of any actuality, or presence, is assembled from environmental facts and emotional stimuli—from those facts and stimuli of which denotations and illocutionary forces are the doubles within statements. The autonomy of sense from denotation (i.e. from the fact) and from the illocutionary force (i.e. from the stimulus) thus implies its autonomy from all that we have good reason to consider as present. Negation exhibits the *untimeliness of sense* [*l'inattualità del senso*], the crack that disconnects it from the 'now'. But there is a complication: without this basic untimeliness, not only would we not have access to the 'not any longer' and the 'not yet', but also, strictly speaking, there would not be a 'now'. However bizarre this may initially seem, it is precisely the split between sense and presence, symbolized by the sign 'not', that establishes the habitual concept of presence (which is unintelligible outside of an oppositional relation to something which by its own nature is always untimely or non-actual). Negation, which on its own certainly does not record time, accounts however for the gap on which the very possibility of recording time depends.

The untimeliness of sense involves a constant *detachment* of the speaker from the environment and the psychic drives. The voids and pauses, that is, the hesitations and postponements that punctuate the experience of the human animal, are symptoms of such a detachment. Hypothetical and counterfactual reasoning, familiarity with falsity, an imponderable intra-specific aggressiveness, the variation of techniques of production and political systems are all rooted in these voids and pauses. The detachment of statements from the environment and psychic drives is reflected within statements by the syntactic connective 'not'. Well before becoming a dignified ingredient of consciousness, *reflection* inhabits the 'system regulated by the image of itself' that is language. Last but not least, the sense of a statement is public, and hence not bound to the mental processes of individuals, only because it is split from presence. What we all share, but nobody owns, is that which, diverging from the 'now', will not let itself be *vorgestellt*, put forward: 'It is for us a matter of that understanding whose peculiar characteristic is in fact that it does not represent its objects and does not presuppose their being represented.'[14] The *public character* of linguistic meanings originates from a temporal mismatch. And since this mismatch finds a grammatical spokesperson in negation, I do not think it is extravagant to conclude that the public character of linguistic meanings is one with our ability to say how things are *not*.

3.4

THE NEUTRALITY OF SENSE

In classical Hebrew there is a vowel, *aleph*, that cannot be pronounced precisely because it is the support of all the letters that can. There is no articulated sound that corresponds to *aleph* but only the beginning of phonatory movement, which can hardly be heard. Omitted because of its excessive simplicity, the phantom-vowel is however indispensable for the formation of every kind of term; not being spoken, it enables us to speak.[15] The negation I call

---

14 Adolf Reinach, 'On the Theory of the Negative Judgment' in Barry Smith (ed.), *Parts and Moments: Studies in Logic and Formal Ontology* (Munich: Philosophia Verlag, 1982[1911]).

15 Daniel Heller-Roazen, *Echolalias: On the Forgetting of Language* (Cambridge, MA: Zone Books / MIT Press, 2005), pp. 21–6.

primary or ontological is in some ways similar to the *aleph*. It ratifies the detachment of linguistic activity from surrounding events and emotional stimuli. More precisely, it expresses the multiple fractures with which such a detachment manifests itself within this very linguistic activity: sense is *not* denotation; sense is *not* the illocutionary force; sense is *not* something present. Ontological negation determines the nature and prerogatives of human discourse in general; however, precisely because of this, it never appears in actual discourses. Ontological negation makes it possible for a meaning to really be a meaning. However, precisely because of this, it exempts itself from any explicit signification. We would not be able to compose or comprehend a statement such as 'the sea is stormy,' if there were not a preliminary 'not' that guarantees the non-identity of sense and denotation (i.e. the independence of the statement from the state of affairs around which it revolves). But the preliminary 'not', just like the *aleph*, carries out its task only as long as it remains unapparent, implied, not proffered.

Ontological negation, the mute vowel at work in every locution, institutes and preserves the *neutrality of sense*. By virtue of the gap that separates it from denotation and the illocutionary force (or, if you prefer, from the facts of the external world and psychic drives), the sense of a statement is always suspended between alternative developments, maintaining a perfect equidistance from them. A given semantic content, for example, the thought of Marco running away from the police, can have *or* not have a denotation, and, thus, can turn out to be true *or* false. The same semantic content can moreover join one *or* the other illocutionary force (order, imploration, oath, wish, etc.) and, once the conjunction has taken place, it can figure *both* as a desirable event ('Marco, I beg you to run away') and as an event to be inhibited ('Marco, I beg you not to run away'). These alternatives, with regard to which the thought of Marco running away preserves its neutrality intact, are however secondary. What really matters is the *equidistance of sense with respect to affirmation and negation*. Suspended between 'yes' and 'no', sense is simultaneously open to both. The semantic content '*p*' remains unvaried in '*p* happens' and '*p* does not happen'; it never identifies with one of the two possibilities. Sense is neutral, that is, liable to both affirmation and (empirical) negation, since it is separated from any form of presence. But the separation of sense from presence is attested to by the negation-*aleph*, by the primary or ontological 'not' every discourse benefits from. The reason why I can say, indifferently, 'Marco runs away' or 'Marco does not run away' is that the thought 'running away of Marco' is *not* actual, that is, it does *not* depend on environmental and psychological circumstances. In short, what grounds the equidistance of sense with regard to affirmation and (empirical) negation is ontological negation, which is unavoidable for the constitution of any kind of sense. The *aleph* that cannot be pronounced, that is, the 'not' inherent to the very act of signifying, is the common ground of the signifying sounds 'yes' and 'no'.

The neutrality of sense dispels a pernicious belief, which has always been dear to those who intend to explain the functioning of verbal language with notions obtained from psychology. I am referring to the belief according to which negating would be equivalent to producing a mental picture of the contrary (by contrary, I mean the term that is the furthest from the one in question within the kind they both belong to: what is bitter, if we are dealing with what is sweet; what is bad, if we are dealing with what is good; etc.). Already criticized in the previous chapter, this belief now loses any remaining plausibility. Let us see why. The same sense is open to both affirmation and negation, without lending towards either. From this follows, however, that the affirmative statement and the corresponding negative statement ('Marco runs away,' 'Marco does not run away') share the same sense (the thought 'running away of Marco'). What is decisive from all angles is the *identity of the semantic content to which affirmation and negation are applied*. When we say 'Marco does not run away,' we continue to talk about the 'running away' event, even if we put it out of play. It therefore does not indicate in any way the contrary of such an event, that is, Marco launching himself at the police; it does not introduce, not even implicitly, a new semantic content. According to Aristotle,[16] the heterogeneity between linguistic negation and the psychological evocation of the contrary (i.e. the existing gap between 'The food is not sweet' and 'The food is bitter') becomes evident as soon as we notice that we are able to negate without difficulty predicates that are entirely devoid of a contrary: for example, the result of a multiplication or the humanity of an Arab. The negation of that which does not have a contrary demonstrates that, in negating, we always do something different from representing the contrary (also and above all in the cases where there is a contrary). This something different amounts to *preserving* a certain semantic content,

16 Aristotle, *On Interpretation*, 23b, 27–32.

in itself neutral, at the same time as we *remove* it; it amounts to exhibiting the original opening of sense to both 'yes' and 'no' precisely when we are privileging only the second direction.

In his notes published under the title *The Big Typescript* (2013[2000]), Wittgenstein observes that, by saying he does not feel any pain, the speaker inevitably evidences his ability to feel it: 'I describe my present state by alluding to something that is not the case.'[17] What matters is clarifying in what way 'my present painless state contain[s] the possibility of pain'[18] or what is responsible for the existence of a logical space shared by affirmation and negation. To this end, Wittgenstein proposes a comparison that is very useful to intuitively depict the neutrality of sense: '"Pain" means the *entire measuring stick*, as it were, and not one of its graduation marks. That it is located on a certain mark is to be expressed by a proposition.'[19]

The propositions 'I feel pain' and 'I do not feel pain' are marks of the same measuring stick, alternative permutations of an identical semantic content. If there were not a measuring stick that associates it with an affirmative proposition, the negative proposition would mean that 'my present state has *nothing to do* with a painful one—as I might say the colour of this rose has nothing to do with Caesar's conquest of Gaul.'[20]

---

17 Ludwig Wittgenstein, *The Big Typescript* (Oxford: Blackwell, 2013[2000]), p. 960.

18 Ibid.

19 Ibid. (emphasis added).

20 Ibid.

Now, the 'entire measuring stick' is sense as yet not compromised, suspended between divergent developments, and neutral with respect to affirmation and negation. Save to add that sense resembles a measuring stick that is not set down on a particular notch only and precisely because it is *not* something present (neither fact nor psychic drive); in other words, because it is delimited, and thus determined, by ontological negation, by the pervasive and yet unmentioned *aleph*.

The 'entire measuring stick' of which Wittgenstein speaks, that is, the neutral sense 'pain', is not a hidden presupposition of the affirmative mark 'I feel pain' and of the negative mark 'I do not feel pain;' it coexists with them, always displaying its autonomy from both. If, succumbing to an embarrassing Kantian verbal tic, someone wished at all costs to claim that the measuring stick is the condition of possibility of the marks, I would not have anything to object. However, I would add that this condition of possibility, being in turn endowed with an immediate phenomenal reality, does not precede but is *juxtaposed* to the developments arising from it. It is juxtaposed to them and, in many cases, it even takes their place; it often happens that we talk about pain without affirming, or negating, that we feel it. The 'entire measuring stick' does not fail as such to prove its worth, to the detriment of the hypothetical marks (whose actual inscription it instead prevents). The yet-uncompromised semantic content, simultaneously open to the 'yes' and the 'no', at times opposes both the 'yes' and the 'no', thereby gaining an outstanding prominence. There are therefore three distinct poles that the speaker has to come to terms with at any moment: neutral sense, affirmed sense and negated sense. When what is at stake is the way of being of our statements, the law of the excluded middle does not hold. Hegel noticed this— although he is now so discredited that Pinker and Sperber do not find him worthy of attention. In the *Science of Logic*, he writes:

> It [the law of the excluded middle] implies that there is nothing that is neither A nor not-A, that there is not a third that is indifferent to the opposition. But in fact the third that is indifferent to the opposition is given in the law itself, namely, A itself is present in it. This A is neither +A nor −A, and is equally well +A as −A. The something that was supposed to be either +A or −A is therefore related to both +A and −A [. . .] The something itself, therefore, is the third which was supposed to be excluded.[21]

The key here is to identify the linguistic games in which the *tertium datur* claimed by Hegel dominates, namely, a sense that maintains unchanged its equidistance from affirmation and negation. On what occasions are we inclined or even obliged to express an A that 'is neither +A nor −A, and is equally well +A as −A'? How can the 'entire measuring stick' become a prominent figure, rather than remaining confined to the background?

---

21 Georg Wilhelm Friedrich Hegel, *Science of Logic* (Amherst, NY: Humanity Books, 1969[1812–16]), p. 438.

3.5

OF THE QUESTION MARK

The neutrality of sense, always safeguarded anew by the negation-*aleph*, is fully unveiled above all in two kinds of discourses: questions and statements that are introduced by the clause 'it is possible that'. I will deal with the singular powers of the question mark presently while postponing an enquiry into the reciprocal implication of the syntactic connective 'not' and the modality of possibility to the next section.

The questions that are relevant to our ends are certainly not those directed at obtaining a description or an account ('What happened yesterday night?', 'When will you go to Madrid?', etc.), in order to increase the number of themes under discussion, but only those that presuppose as a pertinent reply either assent or denial: 'Is it raining?', 'Is Giovanni a traitor?', 'Do you swear you will love me for ever?', 'Is 3+6 equal to 8?', etc. The person being asked 'Is it raining?' will mostly answer with the affirmative assertion 'it is raining' or the negative assertion 'it is not raining.' The question expresses the same sense (in this case, the thought of rain) around which the two possible answers revolve. But when it is accompanied by the question mark, this sense flaunts its intrinsic independence from the act of asserting; well before compromising itself with affirmation or negation, it shows it is already complete and intelligible. Asking is the linguistic game in which the 'entire measuring stick' not yet positioned on a specific mark comes to the fore; the question 'Is it raining?' gives a concrete appearance to the *tertium datur* which, far from leading an underground existence, is invariably juxtaposed to 'it is raining' and 'it is not raining'. Since it is separated from denotation and illocutionary force, *sense always has the logical form of a question*. Its being suspended before divergent developments finds a fully adequate phenomenal equivalent in the graphic sign '?'.

Conferring an autonomous relevance to the neutrality that characterizes all verbal meanings, interrogative sentences prompt us to recognize this neutrality even in sentences that are not interrogative (beginning of course with the answers provided by the person being questioned). In the second of his *Logical Investigations*, entitled 'Negation', Frege insists on the validity of such a generalization: 'The very nature of a question demands a separation between the acts of grasping a sense and of judging. And since the sense of an interrogative sentence is always also inherent to the assertoric sentence that gives an answer to the question, this separation must be carried out for the assertoric sentences too.'[22]

The difference between question and answer is only the external *projection*—that is, the staging made by two connected statements—of a difference that, although it often remains unperceived, is already present within every single assertoric and pragmatic statement. I am obviously speaking about the difference between a sense that is as such neutral and its affirmation/negation. We can express the same point the other way round: in every affirmative or negative statement ('Giovanni is a traitor,' 'Giovanni is not a traitor') there is a component—the A equidistant

---

22 Gottlob Frege, 'Negation' in Peter Geach and Max Black (eds.), *Translations from the Philosophical Writings of Gottlob Frege* (Oxford: Blackwell, 1960[1918–19]), p. 119.

from +A and –A—that can be isolated, and thus distinguished from the other components of the statement, on condition that it is converted into a question ('Is Giovanni a traitor?').

Frege believes that a negative answer does not destroy or transform the sense contained in the corresponding question. If you ask me 'Is 3+6 equal to 8?', I will respond without hesitation and say that '3+6 is *not* equal to 8'. But my negation does not at all modify the thought previously expressed in an interrogative form—although it refutes it—nor does it replace it with a different thought (with, say, '3+6 is equal to 9'). Even when it is proved blatantly false, sense does not lose any consistency; that is, it remains public, objective and understandable for all speakers (whatever their psychological representation might be). Those who are reluctant to accept this crucial point should then accept the idea that the only real sense is a true sense. They also need to shoulder the burden of maintaining, on pain of ridicule, that a question, as soon as it is intelligible, only admits an affirmative answer. Negation does not dissolve the sense to which it applies, because sense, as sufficiently demonstrated by our ability to create interrogative sentences, pre-exists the alternatives true/false and 'yes'/'no', remaining available and indifferent to both poles. Frege writes:

> How, indeed, could a thought be dissolved? How
> could the interconnection of its parts be split up?
> [. . .] To the structure of the thought there corre-
> sponds the compounding of words in a sentence;
> and here the order is in general not indifferent.
> To the dissolution or destruction of the thought

there must accordingly correspond a tearing apart of the words, such as happens, e.g., if a sentence written on paper is cut up with scissors [. . .]. Is this what happens when we negate a thought? No! The thought would undoubtedly survive even this execution of it *in effigy*. What we do is to insert the word 'not', and, apart from this, leave the word-order unaltered. The original wording can still be recognized.[23]

According to Frege, the fact that the 'not' leaves intact the sense of the statement in which it intervenes is proved beyond reasonable doubt by the fact that double negation reproposes the initial statement in an unaltered state. If we are inclined to consider 'it is *not* true that Aldo is *not* a coward' as equivalent to the affirmation 'Aldo is a coward,' it is only because the thought contained in the latter sentence, that is, Aldo's cowardice, is never eroded or deformed by 'Aldo is *not* a coward.' The only way to avoid this conclusion would be to believe that the second negation miraculously regenerates the semantic content that the first negation annuls: but 'a sword that could heal on again the limbs it had cut off'[24] is far too cheap a trick, even for postmodern supporters of the world of magic.

Let me add a small aside, so that we can turn to fields other than linguistics and logic. For Frege, negation never manages to hide the thought on which it intervenes: 'The original wording can still be recognized.' As we will see later (see 5.4), this is precisely the property of the 'not' that Freud open-mindedly makes the most of in his

---

23 Ibid., p. 123 (emphasis added).
24 Ibid., p. 124.

clinical activity. Faced with a patient who maintains 'doctor, the woman in the dream is *not* my mother,' 'in our interpretation, we take the liberty of disregarding the negation and picking out the subject-matter alone of the association';[25] he therefore postulates that the mother is the actual protagonist of the dream whose account he has just listened to. If 'the original wording' were not still 'recognized' after the patient used the 'not', a similar hypothesis would not find any support. Freud only avails himself, in the specific context of psychoanalytic therapy, of a general characteristic of negative statements: their intrinsic conservation of a rigorously neutral sense that, having its most appropriate expression in the corresponding interrogative sentence ('Is the woman in the dream my mother?'), equally lends itself to affirmation.

We know that the question mark exhibits the neutrality of sense. We also know that the neutrality of sense is the product of ontological negation. We therefore need to suppose that the question mark itself is granted and sustained by a preliminary 'not', which is in many ways similar to the Hebrew letter *aleph*. The very possibility of formulating questions depends on the fractures that generally characterize human language: sense is *not* denotation; sense is *not* the illocutionary force; sense is *not* something present. Each interrogation presupposes the detachment of verbal thought from the surrounding states of affairs and from emotional stimuli. It presupposes it and, at the same time, it announces it. The one who asks

---

25 Sigmund Freud, 'Negation' in James Strachey (ed.), *The Standard Edition of the Complete Psychological Works of Sigmund Freud, Volume 19* (London: Vintage, 2001[1925]), pp. 235–9; here, p. 235.

acquires an attitude of *waiting* that is strongly linked to a state of indetermination. And this waiting is nothing other than an exemplary manifestation—irrefutable precisely because it is familiar—of the *untimeliness of sense*, of its diverging from the environmental and psychological 'now'. While a question is certainly based on the negation-*aleph*, it is however also the strategic place where the latter comes closest to the surface of discourse. The interrogative tone of voice signals the latency of the *aleph*, and gives an auditory guise to its persistent omission.

With a slight variation of our point of view, we could say: the question is a bridge between, on the one hand, ontological negation, which reflects the way of being of language considered as a whole, and, on the other hand, empirical negation, through which we rather speak of what at each turn does not happen. Ontological negation —'sense is *not* ever identical with denotation'—precedes and makes possible all interrogative sentences. On the other hand, empirical negation—for example, the answer 'Francesco does *not* have a dog'—follows a particular interrogative sentence, 'Does Francesco have a dog?', and points out that the sense it contains occasionally lacks a denotation. Precisely because it amounts to an intermediate link between two kinds of 'not', the question helps us to untangle a very important problem (already partially discussed in Chapter 2): establishing whether the relation between negation and affirmation is symmetrical or asymmetrical, and whether the 'yes' and 'no' share the same logical level. Unilaterally cheering for either of these conjectures can well procure a beneficial adrenalin rush— as might happen at a derby match—but does not take us far. It seems to me that the solution to this problem is a hybrid one, which can even take on a paradoxical undertone. Let us first consider the contrasting answers that can be given to a question. The (empirical) negation 'it is not raining' and the affirmation 'it is raining' are certainly symmetrical and of the same stature, since they apply to neutral sense which is equidistant from both and condensed in the interrogative sentence 'is it raining?'. For each affirmation there is one and only one (empirical) negation; and, vice versa, for each (empirical) negation there is one and only one affirmation. The symmetry between 'yes' and 'no' derives from the neutrality of sense, which the question concretely attests to. But this neutrality—I repeat it again at the risk of boring my readers—presupposes in turn the ontological negation, that is, the systematic splitting of sense from presence (from the surrounding states of affairs and from emotional stimuli; from denotation and from the illocutionary force). Ontological negation ('sense is not denotation') is openly asymmetrical with respect to any kind of affirmation: its imaginary counterpart, that is, 'sense is denotation,' would in fact disown the very existence of verbal language and, thus, even its own validity as a particular linguistic phenomenon. The hybrid and even paradoxical solution I hinted at above is roughly as follows: the undeniable *symmetry* between affirmation and empirical negation ('It is raining,' 'It is not raining') is founded on the *asymmetrical* position that rests with a 'not' that is so basic as to be one with speech itself.

3.6
THE 'NOT' AND THE POSSIBLE

What is valid for the question is also by and large valid for the modality of the possible. When we say 'it is possible that it is raining' or 'it is possible that Giovanni is a traitor,' we evidence a meaning *as* pure meaning, unconnected to denotation and the illocutionary force, still exempt from confirmation or denial and suspended between truth and falsity. This is thus not very different from what we do when we ask 'is it raining?' or 'is Giovanni a traitor?' In addition to being related by some evident analogies, the two kinds of statements refer to each other, and, in many cases, even turn out to be interchangeable: in formulating a question about an event *y*, by the same token we inscribe *y* in the field of the possible; reciprocally, in ventilating the possibility of *y*, we are already putting *y* under the sign of the question mark.

The possible, just like the question, expresses the neutrality of sense, that is, the 'entire measuring stick' without marks dear to Wittgenstein, as well as the A as different from +A and −A that Hegel drew attention to. The independence of verbal thought from facts and psychological drives, which is undeniable yet only implicit in assertions and pragmatic statements, fully emerges when this thought is accompanied by the clause 'it is possible that'. If, on the one hand, the modal operator produces a very specific discourse, endowed with unmistakable requisites, on the other, it brings to light a trait shared by all discourses. Like the graphic sign '?', the modality we are dealing with offers a phenomenal equivalent of the *logical form* that always and in any case pertains to linguistic sense. The possible is any meaning '*p*' (e.g. 'feeling pain'), since it *provides us with the possibility* to assert '*p* happens' or '*p* does not happen' ('I feel pain,' 'I do not feel pain'). The possible is the semantic content that remains identical in affirmation and negation, thus revealing its preliminary availability to both. On close inspection, the statement 'it is possible that *p*' limits itself to declaring '*p* is a neutral sense'. But insofar as there is no sense worthy of the name that is not neutral, we need to acknowledge that *every* sense is something possible and, vice versa, that the possible refers only to the way of being of sense. Using the jargon of medieval logicians, handbooks rush to explain that the modality of the possible is *de dicto*, not *de re*, given that it concerns the characteristics of the sentence of which it is part, and not those of the thing or the fact around which the sentence revolves. This is an uncontestable explanation but it is also ungenerous to the point of overlooking what matters the most. The possible is indeed *de dicto* but that is because it illustrates a property of *saying in general* and not only of certain particular *dicta* about which we do not yet know whether they denote an actual state of affairs. Showing clearly the neutrality of sense, that is, the very nature of linguistic signification, the modal operator is not simply *de dicto* but also *de essentia dicendi*.

Pointing out the several threads that link statements on the possible to interrogative statements is only an introductory step. Far from hiding their divergences, their family resemblance is the background against which these stand out distinctly. Those who wish firmly to seize the specific status of the modality of the possible need to take an interest in everything that distinguishes it from its companion, the question.

Let us start with a particular yet decisive aspect. We have seen that sense, in never matching environmental events and psychological stimuli, is not something *present*. The meanings of our sentences cannot be assimilated to reactive signals precisely because they preserve a constant detachment from the 'now'. In the linguistic game of asking, this temporal discrepancy is manifested as the *waiting* for an answer, and thus in the interval between two statements. It is however a matter of a faulty and even misleading manifestation. The untimeliness inherent *to* words is positioned *outside of* words; it coincides with the more or less long silence that follows 'Do you love me?' and precedes 'I love you' or 'I do not love you.' Moreover, putting an end to the waiting, the answer seems to fill the gap between sense and presence. We therefore have the—erroneous yet tenacious—impression that such a gap is incidental and temporary. Things change if we say 'It is possible that you love me.' The separation of the verbal meaning from the 'now' (a separation each locution benefits from) is exhibited here within an individual statement. The modal operator introjects *within language* the interval loaded with uncertainty that, in the case of asking, extends itself between the conclusion of an utterance and the beginning of the one that follows. Possible is synonymous with *untimely* and not-present. So that, in 'it is possible that you love me,' the temporal discrepancy constitutes the very theme of the discourse, rather than transpiring indirectly at its margins, as a collateral effect. And given that 'It is possible that you love me' is not a preparatory stage in view of one of the two opposite assertions 'You love me' or 'You do not love me,' but has the stature of an autonomous evaluation (able to deactivate the alternative between these assertions), the temporal discrepancy designed by modality is not reversible. The waiting is no longer a mere setback, or a parenthesis to be quickly closed, but becomes something permanent. Only the possible, not the question, thus attests to the permanent *untimeliness of sense*.[26] But have we not observed on numerous occasions that the primary function of negation lies precisely in its expressing this untimeliness, in giving voice to the gap between meanings and presence? If this is the case, it seems to me legitimate to suppose straightaway that the possible is perfectly coextensive with the 'not': any attempt to specify which of the two is the shadow and which the body, the protagonist and the *alter ego*, would be futile.

What we have just said already enables us to glimpse the fundamental difference between the possible and the

---

26 It would be wrong to believe that the untimeliness of sense is at work only where the latter refers to a future event. The error here lies in confusing the temporality of facts of the external world with the temporality of linguistic meanings. The naval combat that perhaps will take place tomorrow, which Aristotle discusses in a well-known passage (see *On Interpretation*, 19a, 23–32), is untimely, that is, possible, because it has not yet taken place. On the contrary, the sense of a statement (even in the present tense, for instance, 'Your dog is biting a child') is untimely, that is, possible, *insofar as it takes place*, namely, insofar as it already exists as sense, since, at the very moment when it takes place, it *can* be affirmed or negated, it *can* turn out to be true or false. Unlike events, which are potential only if they are in the future, sense is *always* potential, and it is so precisely on condition of being really expressed. We could also quip: each verbal meaning, separated as it is from the 'now', resembles a naval combat that perhaps will be fought tomorrow.

question. By marking the division between the utterance of which it is nonetheless a part and the environmental and psychological 'now', the modal operator *condenses* in a single statement all the elements that, in asking a question, remain instead separated from each other, since they are distributed over different statements: (a) the question understood in a strict sense, which singles out a sense that is still neutral; (b) the prospective affirmative answer; (c) the prospective negative answer. In short, 'It is possible that it is raining' absorbs in itself that which was earlier divided between 'Is it raining?', 'It is raining' and 'It is not raining'—that is, both the suspension instituted by the question mark and the two antipodal replies. However, we have to understand how this condensation is carried out and which new elements it introduces with respect to the starting point. The question 'Is it raining?' requires completion: either 'It is raining' or 'It is not raining.' And this completion marks the passage from the neutrality of sense to its unilateral qualification. On the contrary, 'it is possible that it is raining' is a self-sufficient statement which does not need any integration, and whose peculiar characteristic is that it includes in itself both 'It is raining' and 'It is not raining,' without privileging either of the two options. But what is responsible for the inclusion, and above all the coexistence, of both answers? When the possible is at stake, affirmation and negation figure as the latent albeit inescapable prerogatives of neutral sense, and no longer as the turning point at which neutrality fails. The permanent untimeliness of the semantic content also infects the 'yes' and 'no': if they subsist simultaneously it is precisely in virtue of their detachment from the 'now'. As soon as they are transposed into a modal statement, the answers 'It is raining' and 'It is not raining' are invested with the suspension that previously concerned only the question 'Is it raining?' Rather than amounting to the circumscribed and incomplete background of a real affirmation or real negation, the neutrality of sense now surfaces as the *possibility* of affirmation and the *possibility* of negation.

The notion of the possible always contains in itself, among its structural components, the 'not', the defective eventuality—in the same way in which the notion of the body analytically contains the property of extension. When we say 'It is possible that you love me,' we also say at the same time 'It is possible that you do *not* love me.' It is not a matter of a mere coexistence between a positive and a negative inclination, of an *et-et* such as: You may love me and you may not love me. We are, rather, dealing with a binding inference or, better, with a sheer implication: *If* it is possible that you love me, *then* it is possible that you do not love me. Aristotle writes:

> However, it certainly seems that the same thing may be and not be. Thus, for instance, whatever may walk or be cut may not walk or be cut. And the reason for this is that such things as are in this manner possible do not at all times become actual. Both the positive and the negative statements will, therefore, be true in such cases. For that which may walk or be seen may, *per contra*, not walk nor be seen.[27]

While a question is open to both 'yes' and 'no', *the possible is a 'yes' that implies a 'no'*. As long as it is isolated in an interrogative statement, the neutrality of sense works only as the premise of a real cognitive or practical

27 Aristotle, *On Interpretation*, 21b, 12–17.

stance; when instead it takes place in a statement on the possible, this very neutrality becomes, as such, a specific and very complex stance vis-à-vis one's vital context, elevated to the status of an incisive judgement. If we accept the similitude proposed by Wittgenstein, we should say that, where the modal operator appears, the 'entire measuring stick', that is, neutral sense, also constitutes (thanks to its ambivalence, and not in spite of it) a *sui generis* mark, able to guide reasoning and action.

According to Aristotle, 'it is possible that the fabric is *not* cut' does not at all contradict 'it is possible that the fabric is cut', since, as we have just seen, the possibility of not being cut is connected from the beginning with the possibility of being cut. In order to obtain a contradictory statement, we need to place the 'not' before the modal operator: 'It is *not* possible that the fabric is cut.' Obviously, this remark is correct. We, however, have to examine the relation between 'It is *not* possible that' and 'It is possible that *not*'. In the first case, we have an ordinary negation: 'It is not possible that the fabric is cut' shares all the characteristics of 'Giacomo does not live in Berlin.' As usual, the 'not' excludes the corresponding affirmation but leaves intact the meaning to which it applies: following our examples, negative statements still speak of the possibility of cutting a fabric and of Giacomo's living in Berlin. It is not difficult to realize that in 'It is possible that the fabric is not cut' there is something more at stake, something different. The negation that is preceded by the modal operator does not limit itself to preserving the meaning 'possibility of cutting the fabric' but *determines* it; not only does it not destroy or alter the semantic content of the affirmative statement 'it is possible that the fabric is cut,' but it is even *incorporated* in it. A negation that does not act on an already given meaning but participates in its very formation, guaranteeing its non-identity with facts (i.e. its *being able not* to have a denotation), has much in common with *ontological negation*. Let me unpack this point. We know that every neutral sense is something possible, and, vice versa, that the possible refers to the way of being of sense. From this follows that the 'not' incorporated in the possible is the same 'not' that, in general, is incorporated in sense. This primary 'not', which makes the possible and sense what they are, is responsible for ratifying the lasting independence of our discourses from states of affairs and psychological stimuli. The negation that takes roots *in* the possible ('It is possible that *not*') relates to the negation *of* the possible ('It is *not* possible that') like ontological negation ('Sense is *not* something present') relates to empirical negation ('Giacomo does *not* live in Berlin').

So far I have tried to show how and why *the possible implies negation*. My argument would however remain incomplete and unfocused if I did not add that the relation between the two terms is bidirectional and thus always subject to a reversal. The premise does not fail to take the place of the conclusion; the outcome generates its *incipit*; the father is the son of his son. The specular inference to the one we discussed is in turn cogent and instructive: *negation implies the possible*. With regard to this second aspect, which is to a large extent intuitive, a few schematic comments should suffice. Their only aim is to corroborate the idea that negation diverges from affirmation precisely because, in its concrete taking place, it always has to present the possible; or, better, because negation alone is able to trace the watershed between the possible and the real, between potential being and actual being.

Let me recall what Wittgenstein writes[28] about the assertion 'I do not feel pain.' The one who utters it accounts for his real status by 'alluding to something that is not the case', that is, he signals that 'my present painless state contains the *possibility* of pain.' Wittgenstein's remark has a general value: when we say 'Giorgio is not at home' or 'Maria, I beg you not to despise me,' we automatically include Giorgio's being at home and Maria's contempt in the catalogue of possible facts. The negated meaning, far from being dissolved by the 'not', preserves its integrity: but it preserves it—and this is crucial—in virtue of its inclusion in the field of action of the modal operator. The possible first appears disguised as what a negation is obliged to mention at the very moment when it decrees its abrogation. While the affirmative statement 'I feel pain' has no need to hint at the opposite eventuality in order to be intelligible, the negative statement 'I do not feel pain' obligatorily refers to something that, while not happening now, could nonetheless happen.[29] What is responsible for the different behaviour of the two statements?

---

28 Wittgenstein, *The Big Typescript*, pp. 959–60.

29 It is easy to verify that, in addition to positing as possible the particular semantic content onto which it is grafted, the 'not' also evokes a set of *undetermined* possibilities, correlated to semantic contents that are completely heterogeneous, and not specifiable at the moment. Let me clarify this: on the one hand, the negative statement 'Giorgio is not at home' refers to the possibility that Giorgio is at home; on the other, it makes us think about the various places where, not being at home, Giorgio *may* be: at the office, getting drunk in a bar, on a sightseeing tour of Afghanistan, etc. But the proliferation of undetermined possibilities, triggered by the 'not', lies outside what interests us here.

Something we already know about. In 'I feel pain' we have a complete juxtaposition between the verbal thought 'feeling pain'—as such equidistant from the 'yes' and the 'no'—and one of its *particular* permutations. Affirmation reduces the 'entire measuring stick' to the mark on which it positions it, or, in other words, it seems to saturate all the potentialities of the semantic content that it expresses: it is always *pars pro toto*. This situation is reversed in 'I do not feel pain': what here comes to light is the neutrality of the sense 'feeling pain', its autonomy from the assertion that is presently underway. Negation makes manifest the non-coincidence between itself, as a specific mark, and the 'entire measuring stick' in which it is inserted: it is always *pars in toto*. We can sum up this issue by means of a rudimentary syllogism. Major premise: the 'not' evidences the neutral sense 'feeling pain'. Minor premise: this neutral sense is entirely equivalent to the modal statement 'It is possible to feel pain.' Conclusion: the 'not' evidences the possible. There is however an important specification to be made, without which we would not grasp the heart of this matter. We have seen that the possibility of feeling pain goes together with the possibility of not feeling it. And yet, in asserting 'I do *not* feel pain' I explicitly declare that the possibility of *not* feeling pain has been realized. As a consequence, the reference to potential sense inherent in 'I do not feel pain' ('It is possible that I feel / do not feel pain') inevitably becomes a reference to the affirmative possibility alone.

The 'entire measuring stick' of which Wittgenstein speaks is the *logical space* that rests with a meaning still suspended between alternative developments. Negation only works if it exhibits, in each of its empirical occurrences, the totality of the logical space of which it is part. But, in exhibiting this totality, negation introduces a *modal distinction* between the region of logical space that it oversees (actual reality) and the region of the same space that rather pertains to affirmation (mere possibility). The totality of logical space, that is, the 'entire measuring stick' of which neutral sense consists presents itself half in actuality (I do not feel pain) and half in potentiality (but I am able to feel it). Such a subdivision is carried out exclusively by the 'not'. The latter does not limit itself to implying potential being but articulates the very difference between actual being and potential being. Negation describes reality on condition of always retracing the borderline, and the juncture, between the real and the possible. The assertion 'The real is *not* thus' is converted into 'The *non*-real is thus,' that is, into 'The possible is *thus*.'

Being familiar with the possible, the human animal is devoted to negation. And vice versa: insofar as it masters negation, the human animal always has to engage with the possible anew. The modal operator and the 'not' imply each other: each derives from the other and, at the same time, institutes it. By way of conclusion, and availing myself of a theoretical dialect that is only slightly different from the one I have used so far, I would like to provide an abbreviated version of this circular relation, which is an eminent element of a plainly *naturalistic* anthropology (i.e. one that is able to acknowledge the importance that some logical structures have in defining the nature of the primate *Homo sapiens*).

The modality of the possible indicates a *disposition* to do or be subject to something. Dispositions are effectively expressed by those adjectives that present the suffix '-able' or '-ible': irascible, breakable, loveable, redoubtable, etc. There is therefore nothing discordant in replacing 'It is possible to access the path' with 'The path is accessible.' But a disposition is really such if and only if it is *not* always realized: I call irascible the one who, in spite of being inclined to outbursts of anger, on many occasions does not get angry. The suffix '-able' or '-ible' is also an indicator of omission and of missing the mark. Fragility pertains to what for the most does not break; amiability to people who long remain unloved; readability to books that in case nobody reads. The attribution of any particular dispo-sition to a grammatical subject presupposes, in turn, a basic disposition that lights up our speech from top to bottom: the disposition to negate. The 'possible that not', that is, the negation located within the modal operator, finds a rigorous equivalent in the adjective 'deniable'. The latter is one among many adjectives that designate a potentiality; it is analogous in all ways to 'documentable' or 'negligible': and yet, the peculiar potentiality designated by 'deniable' contributes to forging the very suffix '-able' or '-ible', which all its brothers share. Deniability is thus nothing other than the *disposition to have dispositions*. With-out it, there would not be anything loveable, believable, enjoyable, but only something that is in fact loved, believed, enjoyed. The point of complete fusion between the modality of the possible and the syntactic connective 'not' is alluded to precisely in *deniability*: indeed, in this disposition negation is fully resolved into a possibility and possibility into a negation.

3.7

THE MISERY OF PSYCHOLOGISM

For better or for worse, all the themes that I intended to discuss in this chapter have been discussed. To conclude, I put before the reader two marginal notes that, as befits travel notes redacted upon reaching one's destination, recall some scenic views glimpsed along the way. The first deals with the clamorous misunderstanding—in many ways similar to Doctor Strangelove's compulsive gesture—with which those who claim to reduce semantics to a branch of psychology entertain themselves. The second briefly returns to the *reflexive* character of negation, that is, its inclination to condense within itself certain distinctive traits of language in general.

Marginal Note I. Negation constitutes the authentic distinction between psychological representations and linguistic meanings. The gap that irrevocably separates a proposition from a mental picture is to be ascribed precisely to negation. The only way in which this distinction can be eluded or neutralized is by setting up a psychologistic interpretation of negation itself. Here is the cornerstone of this interpretation: we claim that negative statements have at their disposal an autonomous content, heterogeneous from that of the corresponding affirmative statements. 'A is not B' would thus equate to 'A is C.' For the supporters of psychologism, negation has the value of a *new affirmation* that is still timid or implicit but rivals the old one and aspires to take its place.

The origin of this conjecture is quite evident. As we will recall, a mental picture, when proven to be illusory, can be refuted only on condition of *replacing* it with a different mental picture, which is responsible for depicting an alternative state of affairs. If I represent psychologically the car accident Andrea was involved in, and then find out that it never happened, I do not have at my disposal any *Vorstellung* able simply to show that the accident did *not* take place: to correct the error, I can only represent Andrea singing at the wheel, or having lunch at a restaurant half-way through his journey or taking out his luggage at the end of it. Now, the badge of honour of the psychologistic interpretation rests on attributing to negation the role that, within pre-linguistic experience, is performed by the supplementary picture aimed at replacing the initial one. The 'not', whose typical prerogative is that of refuting without replacing, is thus conceived as the index, or the instrument, of a replacement. Psychologism finds nothing better to do than extending the peculiar functioning of mental pictures to the syntactic connective that renders pictures and statements incommensurable. What is here mistaken and repressed (even according to the psychoanalytic meaning of the term) is an unquestionable matter of fact, which is such for whoever is able to barely speak a language: by saying 'Andrea did not have a car accident,' I am nonetheless speaking of a car accident, and only of it, not of other activities Andrea would be busy with.

In a 1763 text entitled 'An Attempt to Introduce the Concept of Negative Magnitudes into Philosophy' (briefly mentioned in the previous chapter), Kant warns us against a disastrous yet alluring confusion: mistaking linguistic negation for a 'real opposition' between two independent phenomena, endowed with their own requisites, where each phenomenon tends to elide and supplant the other. For example, think of the relation between attraction and repulsion, pleasure and displeasure, merit and demerit:

> For negative magnitudes [hence, repulsion, displeasure, demerit] are not negations of magnitudes, but something truly positive in itself, albeit something opposed to the positive magnitude [. . .] Falling is not

to be distinguished from rising merely in the way in which 'not a' is distinguished from 'a'. It is rather the case that falling is just as positive as rising [. . .] A real repugnancy only occurs where there are two things, as positive grounds, and where one of them cancels the consequence of the other.[30]

Psychologism builds its nest in the *quid pro quo* that Kant dreaded: it assimilates negation to the 'real opposition'; it flattens the statement 'The room is not bright' onto the statement 'The room is dark'; it suppresses the difference between contradiction and contrariety. The banner of psychologism could well sport the words Stuart Mill dedicated to the principle of non-contradiction:

We also find that light and darkness, sound and silence, motion and quiescence, equality and inequality, preceding and following, succession and simultaneousness, any positive phenomenon whatever and its negative, are distinct phenomena, pointedly contrasted, and the one always absent where the other is present. I consider the maxim in question [that of non-contradiction] to be a generalization from all these facts.[31]

Like the words of all madmen, these too have the virtue of avoiding diplomatic sophistries and half-measures. And those who believe Stuart Mill is only an innocuous nineteenth-century relic should take a look at the most recent handbooks of cognitive psychology.

---

30 Kant, 'An Attempt to Introduce the Concept of Negative Magnitudes into Philosophy', p. 209, p. 215.

31 John Stuart Mill, *A System of Logic, Ratiocinative and Inductive* (London: Parker, 1861), p. 305.

Macroscopic consequences for anthropology and the philosophy of mind follow from the way in which we understand the little word 'not'. Let us consider more closely the idea that negation is a substitutive affirmation. Taking it seriously, one soon feels like asking *what* precisely is affirmed when one utters a negative statement, for example, 'Marco is not running away from the police.' Are we perhaps affirming that Marco is launching himself at the police? Or that he is scratching his head, indifferent to the surrounding mayhem? Or that he is winking at his colleagues in uniform? Or what else? It is impossible to establish it: the meaning of the negative statement will depend entirely on the psychological representations of single individuals. But if the semantic content of which negation would be the bearer is variable, then this should make us think that the semantic content of the starting affirmation is equally variable, since it is itself bound to the mental pictures of the speaker and listener. The instability of the sense of 'Marco is not running away' bears with it the instability of the sense of 'Marco is running away.' Interpreting negation as a substitutive affirmation (or the vector of a 'real opposition') is the cornerstone of the two dogmas of psychologism. According to the first, linguistic meanings, far from having an originally public and impersonal character, would only be an echo of our internal world, or at most the weighted average of several concomitant *Vorstellungen*. The second dogma claims that human nature coincides with the representative activity of an individual mind which needs to be examined in isolation, given the more or less explicit certainty that the relation between several minds does not have any importance in describing such a nature; psychologism will declare with a sly smile that between the minds there is only the air that we breathe.

The dogmas of psychologism are shattered as soon as we restore to the syntactic connective 'not' what belongs to it. It is sufficient to recognize that negation concerns the *same* semantic content around which affirmation revolves, adding nothing to it and subtracting nothing from it. The same meaning is available to those who accept it and those who refuse it. This shows that meaning is neutral; unlike *Vorstellungen*, words preserve a distance from the state of mind of those who utter them. This neutrality turns meaning into a shared resource, a *res publica*, a trans-individual object. Rather than deriving from the mental pictures of individuals, it reorganizes them or even creates them. The sense of a statement whose negation does not affirm something else, that is, does not initiate another different sense, is radically non-psychological. It is only the actual status of the 'not', the gap that divides negation from the 'real opposition', that ensures a reliable foundation for Frege's position:

> The same sense is not always connected, even in the same man, with the same conception. [. . .] This constitutes an essential distinction between the conception and the sign's sense, which may be the *common property of many* and therefore is not a part or a mode of the individual mind. For one can hardly deny that mankind has a common store of thoughts which is transmitted from one generation to another.[32]

Marginal Note II. I have repeatedly stated that negation *expresses* what language *is*. It is not rooted in perceptual disappointments or sentimental turmoil, but refers in the first place to the nature of our speech as such. Here lies the major reason for the failure of psychologistic explanations in this regard. The 'not' is a *reflexive* sign, for it illustrates in shorthand the way of being of all signs. I suggested earlier a comparison that for me—I admit it— is far more than a mere comparison: negation is *the money of language*. Just as money provides an autonomous body to the exchange value—that is, to a quality present in all particular

---

32 Frege, 'Sense and Reference', p. 212 (emphasis added).

commodities—so too the 'not' concentrates in itself characters that belong to each word or, better, precisely those characters that transform a sound or a grapheme into a word. At this stage, finding support (or not) in the set of arguments exposed in this chapter, I would like to establish the reflexive function of negation in a different way. This new formulation is careful not to cancel the previous ones; instead, it specifies and integrates them. Although the still images change at each turn, the camera always films the same object.

What does negation designate? Of what real phenomenon is it the symbol? All in all, of what does its referent consist? The 'not' indicates the *detachment* of linguistic activity from the environment and from psychic drives or, more emphatically, the non-identity of thought and being: the statement is *not* the fact of which it speaks; the statement does *not* coincide with the emotional stimulus that precedes it and accompanies it. We have however observed that the detachment of linguistic activity from the environment and from psychic drives manifests itself within that very linguistic activity through divisions and fractures: sense is *not* denotation (i.e. the verbal double of facts); sense is *not* the illocutionary force (i.e. the verbal double of emotional stimuli). Negation designates these divisions, ratifies them and is their permanent symbol. It provides information about the sense (or meaning: the two terms are for me equivalent) of our discourses—and, importantly, not about one or other particular sense but about the requisites a sense needs to have in principle in order to be really such. The requisites in question are the convex reverse, or the prominent consequence, of the fractures we have just recalled. Insofar as it diverges from both denotation and the illocutionary force, sense is always *untimely*, disconnected from the 'now' of events and desires. It is always *neutral*, that is, open to different configurations, like a measuring stick on which there is not yet any mark. The statements 'Ernesto just loves potato-sack races,' 'Pinocchio hates The Fairy

with Turquoise Hair,' 'Revolution is a dinner party' have completely heterogeneous senses, devoid of a common unity of
measure, but what makes each of them into a meaning, articu-
lable and comprehensible for everybody, is their independence
from the external and internal world, from the surrounding
states of affairs and from mental pictures. Negation is both the
certificate and the guarantee of such independence.

We usually call *analytic* the properties that participate in
determining the meaning of a word; or—but it really amounts
to the same—the properties that can be inferred a priori from
this meaning. When we say 'monk', we also say 'unmarried
man' without having to make an explicit specification. Extension is an unavoidable component of the lexical notion 'body';
if we eliminated it, the notion as a whole would be annulled.
Likewise: having a successor plays a full part in the semantic
content of the syntagm 'natural number'; liquidness is a constitutive element of the concept 'ocean'. Now, it seems to me that
negation is an analytic property—like being unmarried in the case
of 'monk' and having a successor in that of 'natural number'. But
of which word would negation determine the meaning? Obviously, it is not 'star' or 'wolf'. Neither is it names overloaded
with *pathos* such as 'nothingness', 'anxiety' or 'finitude'—despite
what the existentialists down at the bar might believe. So what
is it? I am sure that careful readers have by now guessed the
answer: negation is the analytic property that specifically determines *the meaning of the word 'meaning'*.[33]

---

33 In that programmatic manifesto that is the introduction to *Logical
Investigations*, Husserl never tires of repeating that logical laws are
'ideal', that is, indifferent to psychological representations and empirical
state of affairs, because 'they merely elucidate what is inseparably
asserted in certain verbal or statement-meanings of great generality'
(Edmund Husserl, *Logical Investigations*, Volume I [London: Routledge,
2001(1900–01)], p. 94). We are confronted with 'purely theoretical
truths, ideal in character, rooted in their semantic content and not

It would be bizarre to suppose that a perfectly constituted triangle would only later acquire the property of having three sides. Or that a mountain would gain only at a later stage the prerogative of height. There is no triangle that does not have three sides, nor mountain devoid of height; these are indeed analytic properties. It would be equally bizarre to suppose that, following their formation, verbal meanings then became, among other things, liable to negation. In this way, we lose sight of an essential point: meaning is what it is *because* it includes in itself negation from the beginning. We know that 'not' expresses the detachment of meanings from facts and emotional stimuli, that is, its autonomy from denotation and the illocutionary force. Without this detachment, meaning would not only be faulty or incomplete, it would immediately cease to be a meaning and be reduced to a mere signal. Incidentally, it is this very detachment, exhibited by the 'not' always anew, that imposes the submission of meaning to *use*. Precisely because it is *not* something present, and hence precisely because

---

straying beyond it' (ibid., p. 97). Let me add three interconnected remarks. (*a*) It is easy to realize that the meaning of the words logic deals with ('true', 'false', 'possible', 'necessary', 'deduction', 'contradiction', etc.) is inseparable from the meaning of the word 'meaning'. In order to grasp the former, we need to thematize the latter. The 'ideality' promoted by Husserl amounts to pondering some particular meanings—but, then, starting from them, *all* meanings, including those of 'red' and 'stone'—in the light of what awards them the status of meanings. (*b*) It is even easier to realize, however, that the meaning of the words logic deals with is also, and perhaps in the first place, inseparable from negation. We would not be able to define the semantic content of 'true', 'false', 'possible', etc., without invoking the sign 'not'. (*c*) All this makes us think that the two aspects we have just noted do not limit themselves to being juxtaposed but are indissolubly entwined, and even refer to each other; when the meaning of the word 'meaning' is at play, negation is always at stake; vice versa, when negation is at play, the meaning of the word 'meaning' is at stake.

it is affected by an original negativity, meaning needs to be articulated and specified in variable ways within an expansive constellation of linguistic games. The detachment from the environment and from psychic drives is filled in by the public *praxis* of speakers, by the historically changeable and yet impersonal grammars that regulate it, and certainly not by a belated suture between verbal thought and state of affairs, or even less by a surplus of supporting *Vorstellungen*. The multiple uses of words presuppose the negativity of meaning; the negativity of meaning implies the multiplicity of uses. The primacy of praxis in linguistic communication is based on the peculiar powers of a syntactic connective: it is not up to sociologists but logicians to get their head around this primacy.

Negation is reflexive, not meta-linguistic. It does not set up discourses *on* previous discourses but brings to light a distinctive trait of every discourse, be it of the first, second or another level. The 'not' contributes to determine the meaning of the world 'meaning', and yet it is also a word among others that intervenes in the construction of countless particular meanings. Negative statements ('Antonio is not sick,' 'I order you not to come to Rome,' etc.) evidence the occasional discordance between a specific semantic content and the corresponding denotation (or the illocutionary force that is provisionally attached to it). This *empirical* discordance is registered by the same sign that documents the *ontological* non-identity of the semantic content—whatever it is—with denotation and the illocutionary force—whatever they may be. The reflexive, but not meta-linguistic, vocation of negation transpires precisely in the twofold role—empirical and ontological—it carries out; that is, it transpires in its amphibious or Janus-faced nature. As an integral part of their punctual and circumscribed meaning, negative statements include a term—the humble 'not'—that, above all, concerns the meaning of 'meaning'. From this follows that, being an integral part of countless meanings that are punctual and circumscribed, the meaning of 'meaning' exercises a great influence on the way in which we depict the world and inhabit it, as well as on the shape taken by our actions and passions. The reflexive sign, which illustrates the way of being of all signs, always has an immediate operative effect.

Linguistic praxis heavily exploits certain very concrete tools, devoid of any prestige, whose salient characteristic however amounts to mirroring the very conditions that make linguistic praxis possible. It therefore avails itself of *transcendental tools*, if we wish to use a more intellectual jargon. Among these tools negation stands out for its importance. It is, at the same time, an *element* and a *rule* of signifying: an element, since it contributes to the formation of all kinds of contingent meanings; a rule, since it determines nothing less than the meaning of the word 'meaning'. If we overlook the convergence or, better, the constant superimposition, of element and rule, phenomenon and condition of possibility, empirical plane and ontological plane, we are doomed to miss our typically human *reflexivity*. That is, the torments of self-consciousness and the functioning of that field of experience to which a long tradition has given the cumbersome name of 'spirit' will remain incomprehensible. But who cares? I bet that great successes will be achieved instead in investigating the reflexivity of angels and ticks.

4.
On Plato's *Sophist*

4.1
THE DISCOVERY OF NEGATION IN INFANCY

The use of negation, that is, the ability to speak of facts that do *not* take place or properties that do *not* belong to a given object, elicits the greatest surprise and poses problems of all kinds especially on two occasions: in early infancy, and in Plato's *Sophist*. The difficulty of mastering negative statements and the doubt about their legitimacy make themselves strongly heard both in the course of ontogenetic development and in one of the most prestigious and influential texts of the metaphysical tradition. It is not just a matter of a suggestive albeit casual, and in the end tedious, affinity. What is really at stake is a cogent connection or, if we prefer, a vertiginous game of mirrors. The *Sophist* reconstructs from a theoretical point of view a salient stage of ontogenesis, returning for a moment to the situation of infancy in which nothing is less obvious than the 'not'. Vice versa, the child's initial incapacity to say how things are *not* throws light on some of the most tortuous passages of the Platonic dialogue: in particular, it helps us understanding why Parmenides' ban on speaking of what is *not* seems at first sight so *natural*.

The difference between these two cases is evident. A child who begins speaking endeavours to *access* negation, testing its prerogatives by means of increasingly complex experiments, halting conjectures and successive rectifications. On the other hand, the two protagonists of the *Sophist*—the Stranger and Theaetetus—attempt to *justify* a negation that, although it is already on everybody's lips, remains enigmatic with regard to its functioning and meaning. But does the justification of a linguistic practice, that is, the recovery of the conditions that make it possible, not perhaps equate with a reflexive redoubling of the ways in which it is concretely accessed? The logical and ontological dilemmas that need to be disentangled in order to come to terms with expressions such as 'a house that is not big' or 'Paolo is not good' coincide to a great extent with the cognitive obstacles that a child has to overcome when he enunciates these expressions for the first time. Identifying in infancy the raw matter of metaphysical enquiries and in metaphysical enquiries an oblique repetition of infancy—this is a central theme for orienting ourselves in the discussion of non-being and negation that takes place in the *Sophist*. Clearly, this is not the only central theme, and perhaps not even the most prominent; but neither is it the weakest or the least fruitful.

Using an impressive amount of empirical data, the researches of Piaget and his collaborators on the ontogenetic formation of the principal logical structures show that the child's language is characterized, at least until the age of seven or eight, by a 'systematic disequilibrium favouring affirmations, since affirmations constitute the more natural and spontaneous behaviours while negations, which are far more difficult to construct and use, are always delayed'.[1]

When a child intends to evidence an extraneousness, a disparity, a contrast, he always avails himself of affirmative locutions: to the term 'beautiful' he opposes terms endowed with their own autonomous semantic content, for example, 'stained', or 'broken' or 'disgusting', and not the negative syntagm 'not beautiful'. He is still unable to refer to the objects that do not fall within class A (e.g. that of birds) as to what simply *is not* A, and indicates them by appealing to their positive identity: this object *is*, rather, a B (tiger), that other object *is* a C (flower), etc.

According to Piaget, the 'systematic disequilibrium favouring affirmations' derives from the temporary submission of verbal discourse to pre-linguistic forms of cognition. Utterances in infancy are nothing else than an appendix, or a dependent variable, of perceptive and sensorimotor experience. And such experience does not grant any space to the 'not'. One sees, touches, hears what is present, not what is missing: 'On a perceptual level, we only grasp

---

1 Piaget, *Recherches sur la contradiction*, II, p. 164.

positive characters and negation is not a relevant aspect.'[2] An interrupted or hesitant movement is anything but the negation of a movement. It is thus mistaken to confuse the return to the starting point that follows the failure of an action with the refutation of the latter; the new beginning does not elide the previous performance but is added to it. As is well known, perception and sensorimotor activity are the matrix of mental pictures. We could thus also say that language in infancy is not familiar with negation because it remains bound to the iconic dimension. Recall Wittgenstein's blunt judgement which we discussed at length in the previous chapter: 'So, can one negate a picture? No. And in this lies the difference between picture and proposition.' Well, there is a stage in ontogenesis during which propositions, taking on the status of pictures, turn out to be undeniable. Of course, the speech of a preschool child contains signals of refusal and reticence, attempts to remove by means of words the obstacles in the way of one's aim, protests against the absence of the desired object, imitations of the prohibitory 'no' the child hears from adults.[3] But these are reactions caused by environmental circumstances and external events. What is still not present is an *endogenous* negation: that is, a negation that, constituting a physiological and pervasive element of

---

2 Ibid., p. 165.

3 See Bertrand Russell, *Human Knowledge: Its Scope and Limits* (New York: Simon & Schuster, 1948); Lois Bloom, *Language Development: Form and Function in Emerging Grammars* (Cambridge, MA: MIT Press, 1970); Virginia Volterra and Francesco Antinucci, 'Negation in Child Language: A Pragmatic Study' in Elinor Ochs and Bambi B. Schieffelin (eds), *Developmental Pragmatics* (New York: Academic Press, 1979), pp. 281–303.

linguistic praxis, inheres *de jure* in any statement simply because it really is a statement.

In Plato's dialogue, just like in our infancy, what prevails at the beginning is a thinking that can only affirm. The limit of this kind of thinking becomes manifest as soon as it is called to account for an undisputable matter of fact: the existence of the sophist. The latter is a human type whose being in the world is characterized by a specific use of language. The sophist speaks falsehoods, prepares rich verbal images that are entirely fictitious (*eídola legómena*, i.e. statements that aspire to be icons, or even paintings)[4] and produces with his sentences appearances to which nothing corresponds. But saying falsehoods is equivalent to speaking about what is *not*. It is here that the problem of negation arises, which at first sight appears irresolvable. What does the phrase 'that which is not', *to me on*, refer to? What value do we have to attribute to the *me*—the 'not'—that associates this phrase to all the countless phrases with which we register an absence or a privation ('He is not at home,' 'He is not rich,' etc.)? For those who—being children or philosophers taught by Parmenides—assumed up to that moment that we can speak only of what is, answering these questions causes a great embarrassment: 'The truth is, my friend, that we are faced with an extremely difficult question. This "appearing" or "seeming" without really "being", and the saying of something which yet is not true—all these expressions have always been and still are deeply involved in perplexity.'[5]

---

4 Plato, *Sophist*, 234b1–c 7.

5 Ibid., 236e.

'Have always been and still are': it goes without saying that Plato is targeting the past philosophical tradition, but it does not seem to me inadequate to pay attention to a second kind of past, the ontogenetic one, of which each member of our species is a direct witness and potential historiographer.

There is an aspect we should not overlook. Negation does not have a prominent role in the discourses of the sophist. On the other hand, it is indispensable to define the nature of these discourses (their revolving around what is *not*), and, even more, to understand the form of life of those who utter them. In his lectures on the *Sophist* held in Marburg in 1925, Heidegger repeatedly insists on the existential motivation that animates the logical-linguistic enquiry to which the Stranger and Theaetetus are devoted: 'There is concretely, in sophistical comportment, an onto-logical unification of *léghein* [saying] with *pseudós* [false], i.e. with *me on* [. . .] The sophist is the factual existence of *me on* itself.'[6]

Well before defining a state of affairs ('Theaetetus does not fly,' 'Giorgio is not a Marxist'), negation is needed to describe a particular use of language and the ethical attitude correlated with it. For Plato, the 'not' can account for the activity of a very seductive man who, walking the streets of the city, speaks of nothing with statements which are nevertheless well-formed and endowed with meaning. But the Sophist's discourse is not the only one that can be analysed exclusively through negation. We also need to refer to the 'not' to explain the linguistic game of

---

6 Martin Heidegger, *Plato's 'Sophist'* (Bloomington: Indiana University Press, 1997[1992]), p. 398.

irony, which is very often based on asserting the opposite of what actually is. Or to decipher the jargon with which the opportunist, as another 'factual existence of *me on*', works in the shadows, that is, handles the as-yet-impalpable possibilities from which he hopes to profit, as if they were the most solid and reliable entities. Furthermore, the 'not' is necessary to reconstruct the ethical-linguistic behaviour of those cautious and sceptical individuals, proliferating epidemically in the so-called postmodern age, who fill their days with negative actions such as abstaining, renouncing, omitting, postponing (actions on which I will dwell later). Let me repeat the point we need not to lose sight of: according to the *Sophist*, negation above all succeeds in clarifying certain linguistic uses, that is, something we do with words. Provided for a moment that this is the case, we need to ask how the child's acquisition of negation takes place. Here is a not-too-unlikely hypothesis: the child begins to say 'not' in order to clarify what he himself does when he complains about a pain he does not feel or speaks about his fights with an imaginary friend. He thus begins to say 'not' to reflexively illustrate the texture of some linguistic games he has already practised; or, if you prefer, to document the verbal deeds of the sophist that dwells in him. Let it be clear that these are only incidental remarks.

Showing at every turn of sentence the 'unification of *léghein* [. . .] with *me on*', negation brings with it an idea of logos that clashes with that envisaged by Parmenides. Disregarding the Parmenidean warning 'Never let this prevail—that that which is not is'[7] is not different from calling into question the intuitive certainties of thought

---

7 Plato, *Sophist*, 237a8.

in infancy, and correcting the 'systematic disequilibrium favouring affirmations' that serves as its banner. Readers of the Platonic dialogue will recall the hesitation the Stranger succumbs to when he is obliged to dispute with Parmenides, aware as he is of running the risk of being accused of 'parricide' (*patraloía*):[8] 'We shall find it necessary in self-defense to do violence to that pronouncement of father Parmenides, and establish by main force that what is not, in some respect has being.'[9]

But the symbolic killing of the philosophical father resembles in many ways an abrupt discharge from the cognitive procedures that prevail in the early years of life. Putting this into a truculent expressive register, we could say that the parricide is also, at the same time, an infanticide. From both the ontogenetic and theoretical standpoints, the irruption of the 'not' in human life amounts to a traumatic event, given that it bears witness to the splitting of verbal thought from presence, that is, to its uncanny autonomy from the environmental states of affairs perceived in each particular instance. From both standpoints, we have to confront the passage from an entirely positive speech, without gaps or voids, to a speech in which all that is said [*detto*] can always be retracted [*disdetto*].

4.2
DRIFTING AND LANDING

What does the locution 'that which is not', *to me on*, mean then—a locution the Stranger uses to name the set of facts and objects evoked by the false discourse of the sophist?

---

8 Ibid., 241d2.
9 Ibid., 241d5–7.

'That which is not' shares the logical form of countless other negative expressions that punctuate everyday conversation: 'He is not chaste,' 'He is not quick,' 'I do not love him,' etc.; it also causes the same headaches. Its merit lies in exhibiting the otherwise unapparent structure of these far more familiar expressions. Hence, interrogating the meaning of *me on* is the main way of grasping negation in general. Those who sense a gap between 'that which is not chaste' and 'that which is not' are, of course, not wrong. While in the first case an individual predicate is at stake, in the second the very possibility of predicating is at play. But the unquestionable disparity between the two phrases is only unveiled against the background of their analogy. The lack of being and the lack of chastity, however different they may appear in relation to everything else, are nevertheless linked and made commensurable by the syntactic connective 'not', thanks to which we are able to speak about both. For Plato, what is decisive is the circular relation between the ontological and linguistic planes, the thought of non-being and the subtraction of a particular attribute from a grammatical subject. But we also need to add that the circular relation is established by negation, and thus by a peculiar requisite belonging to one of the two planes: the linguistic.

The central part of the *Sophist* is delimited by two different explanations of the meaning of 'that which is not'. The first is immediately disappointing; it turns out to be so contradictory that it refutes itself at the very moment it is stated. Much against its intention, this ruinous hypothesis corroborates Parmenides' position while also laying out the reasons that lead the child to keep away from negative expressions. The second explanation of the 'not' appears instead to be adequate and reliable, although it is the point of arrival of an argumentative itinerary that is quite convoluted. It is only this second explanation that manages to settle accounts with Parmenides and provide information on how the overcoming of an ontogenetic threshold is accomplished by every linguistic animal. For the time being, let us limit ourselves to considering the two extreme poles—that is, the initial impasse and the final outcome—without paying attention to the reflections and debates that take place in between. However, we need to put forward a warning that should by now be almost superfluous. Although they refer especially to the grandiose syntagm 'that which is not', according to Plato, both the erroneous and the adequate solution concern particular negations which we continuously encounter, devoid of any philosophical appeal, that is, the usual 'He is not chaste' and 'He is not quick;' this confirms the commensurability of all the locutions in which the 'not' is at work.

The fallacious conjecture—which the Stranger examines just enough to reveal its utter inconsistency[10]—follows a spontaneous inclination of thought in infancy: believing that negation has its own meaning, independent from that of the corresponding affirmation. Let me clarify this: on the basis of such a conjecture, 'The armchair is not red' would be an implicit equivalent or an awkward disguise of 'The armchair is green.' Plato sometimes uses the word *enantion*, 'contrary', to designate the supposed autonomous meaning of negation.[11] But he uses it in a very broad sense. In the *Sophist*, contraries are not only

---

10 See ibid., 237a–242b.

11 Ibid., 257b3–9.

the furthest terms contained within the same kind of reality (e.g. bitterness and sweetness, if we are dealing with taste) but also terms that, unrelated with regard to their kind, radically oppose each other even if they do not have points of contact or, better, precisely because of that. Let us now turn to the case that attracts and worries the two interlocutors prone to commit parricide: the negative syntagm 'that which is not'. If each negation has at its disposal an autonomous meaning, split from that expressed by the affirmation, what will the specific meaning of the syntagm in question be?

A few lines of the dialogue are sufficient to ascertain that the alleged semantic autonomy of negation is here turned into a negation of semantics as a whole. 'That which is' in fact concerns all the possible contents of our discourse: kinds, properties, accidents and number. Insofar as it is their *enantion*, i.e. their specular opposition, 'that which is not' does not therefore have any kind, or property, or accident or number. In short: negation lacks any sort of meaning. The 'absolute non-being' that Plato calls *to medanós on* implies the pure and simple vanishing of language, the dissolution of the grammatical components of a statement (nouns, verbs, adjectives, deictics, etc.), and the catastrophe of verbal thought. 'That which is not' cannot be predicated of anything, or figure as a subject capable of being awarded a predicate. It (but saying 'it' is already too much in its regard) eludes the *léghein* to such an extent that it cannot even be refuted, since in order to refute it we would have to qualify it or at least name it. The contrary of 'that which is' is resolved into the contrary of speaking. 'You see the inference then. One cannot legitimately utter the words, or speak or think of that which is not in itself and for itself [*to me on autó kath'autó*]: it is unthinkable, not to be spoken of or uttered or expressed.'[12]

Later on in the dialogue, Plato observes that 'this isolation of everything from everything else means a complete abolition of all discourse':[13] the disintegration of the relation between linguistic signs gives rise to a *léghein medén*, a 'saying nothing'. But the first and most serious 'isolation' amounts to separating the sense of the negative statement from that of the affirmative statement. The *léghein medén*, or 'saying nothing', is the only adequate equivalent of the *medanós on*, or 'absolute non-being'. And vice versa: the 'absolute non-being' perfectly overlaps with the non-being of discourse. However, the terms 'equivalent' and 'overlap' remain vague: the *léghein medén* and the *medanós on* are in fact the same thing; they are never discernible and always interchangeable.

The fallacious conjecture does not fail to produce inconsistencies and nonsense even when we deal with particular and circumscribed negations, such as 'It is not red' or 'It is not big.'[14] Let us suppose that, having a meaning that is independent from 'It is big,' 'It is not big' is synonymous with 'It is small' or 'It is of the right size.' If this were the case, we would not have a negation at all but a new affirmation. This is what happens to language in infancy without however resorting to any grammatical simulation: as we learn from Piaget's investigations, a child immediately identifies that which is not a bird with a positively

---

12 Ibid., 238c8–11.

13 Ibid., 259e4–5.

14 See ibid., 257b6–7.

determined object, for example, a tiger or a flower. Rather than limiting himself to deactivating the predicate of which he is speaking, the child already delineates a further predicate which is aimed at taking the place of the former. Those who claim that negation is the sign of the contrary, the *enantíon*, must ultimately conclude that negation is impossible. Better said, that it is twice impossible, for different albeit convergent reasons. If we dare to say 'that which is not', we are not saying anything. If, on the other hand, we are happy with a more modest 'It is not big,' we are not really negating but replacing one affirmation with another. Either we do not speak any longer or, in speaking, we are always confronted with a full semantic content, one that is self-sufficient and saturated. In both cases, negation is put out of play, reduced to a false movement or a mere semblance. In virtue of this twofold impasse, we remain at the mercy of a language that, preserving the predilections and the idiosyncrasies of infancy, still conforms to Parmenides' warning.

Following a series of vicissitudes, which I will briefly discuss later, what amends the inaugural error is the introduction of the category of *héteron*, 'different'. Let us read the passage from the *Sophist* that discusses the final—and incontrovertible according to Plato—result of an inquiry on negation:

> STRANGER. When we speak of 'that which is not' [*opótan to 'me on' légomen*], it seems that we do not mean something contrary [*enantíon*] to what exists but only something that is different [*héteron*]

> THEAETETUS. How?

STRANGER. In the same way that when, for example, we speak of something as 'not tall', we may just as well mean by that phrase 'what is equal' as 'what is short', mayn't we?

THEAETETUS. Certainly.

STRANGER. So, when it is asserted that a negative signifies a contrary of the negated term, we shall not agree, but admit no more than this—that the negations '*me*' and '*ou*' used as prefix indicate something different from the words that follow, or rather from the things designated by the words pronounced after the negative.[15]

Here is the crucial point in the history of philosophy *and* in ontogenetic development: rather than forging a new meaning, opposed to the one enclosed in the affirmation, the syntactic connective 'not' refers back to a difference that is not positively specifiable, to an other-from-*x* that becomes intelligible only taking into account the salient traits of *x*. While the *enantíon* initiates a second and well-defined lexical entity ('black', if we were talking about 'white'), the *héteron* only indicates the difference between the lexical entity from which we started ('white') and the totality of conceivable lexical entities. It indicates difference as such, not something different; the pure *relation* of otherness, and not the concrete term in which it is materialized at each turn. The *héteron* is always undetermined: the statement 'this drink is not bitter' does not insinuate that the drink is sweet or sour or perhaps insipid but

---

15 Ibid., 257b3–15.

signals the empty non-identity between its taste and that 'bitter' which remains the only semantic content to be really in question. In an essay on the *Sophist* that is in many ways commendable, Dixsaut has clarified this aspect: 'Thinking what is not-just does not mean thinking what is unjust, or thinking nothing, or thinking everything except for what is just, but necessarily referring to what is just by thinking *its* other.'[16]

I will extensively deal with the characteristic properties of the *héteron* in the next sections. However, it seems important to provide here a synthetic sketch of this notion. These are just the basics to understand what we are discussing and what is really at stake. Given that they will be resumed and developed later, these hints are akin to setting an appointment. The *héteron* originally manifests itself in the relation between linguistic signs: each sign is different from the other signs, but it is precisely this difference that enables it to combine with them in a statement endowed with sense. To form a discourse, it is necessary to use elements that are heterogeneous. 'Paolo' links with 'good' in the assertion 'Paolo is good' only because the two terms are *héteroi*, different: in other words, only because 'Paolo' is *not* 'good'. If the word 'being' denotes anything about which we can have a discourse or a thought, according to Plato, non-being dwells in the *non-identity of the parts that compose discourse and thought*. Coinciding with the negative-differential relations

---

16 Monique Dixsaut, 'La Négation, le non-être et l'autre dans le "Sophiste"' in Pierre Aubenque (ed.), *Études sur le "Sophiste" de Platon* (Naples: Bibliopolis, 1991), pp. 167–213; here, p. 200.

between individual meanings, 'that which is not' is located within 'that which is'—it is always rooted in its folds and partakes in shaping it. The *me on* is not only sayable but even constitutes the unavoidable outline of our saying. Moreover, it is easy to verify that the *héteron* is also applied to the very sign 'being': as an atomic element of a sentence, the latter is itself different from the countless signs with which it is combined. 'Being' is not 'stone' nor 'movement' nor 'rage', etc.; hence, 'stone', 'movement' and 'rage' need to be rightly considered as something other than 'being', as temporary embodiments of non-being.

Having thus solved the enigma of the *me on*, we can now explain actual negation. In negative statements, the pervasive difference that generally qualifies the relation between signs is condensed into an autonomous sign, the 'not', whose function is splitting a particular predicate from a particular subject. When we say 'Paolo is not beautiful,' 'Paolo', which as a sign is already *héteron* with respect to 'beautiful', is for a second time separated from this attribute: the difference between 'Paolo' and 'beautiful' is now inscribed in the semantic content produced by the combination of signs, that is, it is an element of the reality depicted by the statement as a whole. The interstitial *héteron* becomes prominent when it is a matter of showing how things are not. However, we should not overlook the fact that the conversion of 'is beautiful' into 'is not beautiful' presupposes the basic heterogeneity of 'beautiful' and 'just', 'hot', 'wise', etc. The negative predicate 'is not beautiful' refers in fact to everything that from the beginning *is not* 'beautiful', hence to different-from-beautiful (into which 'just', 'hot', 'wise', etc. all flow). The *héteron* is a *disjunction that correlates*, but also, in reverse order, a *relation that disjoins*. As a disjunction that correlates, it enables the combination of words in a statement: because of this, we need to include it in the conditions of possibility of articulated discourse. On the other hand, as a relation that disjoins, the *héteron* gives rise to the specific logical operation of negation. There is a strong link between these two sides, and even a sort of specularity: the way in which discourses are formed *implies* the use of the 'not'; the use of the 'not' *recapitulates* the way in which discourses are formed.

4.3
COMPLEMENTARY CLASSES

At the beginning of this chapter, I have claimed that the argumentative strategy elaborated by Plato in order to *account for* negation mirrors the steps taken by a child at the time when he *accesses* negation with difficulty. I now add that this harmony between philosophical justification and ontogenetic access reaches its climax—and finally presents itself as clear evidence—precisely thanks to the notion of *héteron*. Piaget has no doubts: language in infancy gains an increasing familiarity with negative statements as soon as it is able to single out, with regard to each individual meaning, a counterpart whose only requisite is that of being something *different*. Initially, what gains prominence is an 'intuitive kind of otherness',[17] expressed by the formulas 'the others' or 'all the rest'. These formulas have a lot in common with deictics: like the terms 'this' or

---

17 Jean Piaget and Bärbel Inhelder, *The Early Growth of Logic in the Child* (Abingdon: Routledge, 1964[1959]), p. 130.

'there', they limit themselves to indicating something without describing it. While playing, or when carrying out a task assigned by an adult, the child says loudly: 'The pears go in the basket, the different things out;' 'All the big ones here, the others there;' 'The round ones to the left, the rest to the right.' But this 'intuitive otherness' is only a vague background. The *héteron* accomplishes a crucial role in ontogenesis, actually preparing the ground for the operations of the 'not', when it ceases to be a mere deictic and claims to designate a *class* of entities. Even better: when it gives a decisive contribution to the very constitution of a logic of classes.

Piaget's investigations attest that, at around the age of five, the child begins to regularly identify for each group of identical or similar objects a *complementary class* in which he gathers the objects that do *not* belong to the group in question. If ducks are included in class A, that which is *héteron* with respect to ducks will converge in the complementary class A′. It goes without saying that A and A′ support each other: neither can be thought in the absence of the other. But there is more: the group-duck is transformed into a class *sensu stricto*, that is, into a rigorously delimited collection, only in virtue of its relation with the complementary class. From a genetic standpoint, the first authentic class is the complementary one, given that it alone has right away at its disposal an unequivocal border. There is however a thorny problem with regard to the extension of A′. There are two main possibilities we need to bear in mind. First: for a given period, the child tends to include A (ducks) and A′ (not-ducks) into a class B of a higher level (birds). In this case, the complementary class A′ collects entities that are different from ducks that have, however, the prominent property of being birds. Piaget and Inhelder write:

> There is a class A′ (= B minus A) that can be defined positively for its own characters [. . .] but that can also be defined negatively or for its mere complementarity in B (A′ = the Bs that are not-A). If this second eventuality prevails, there is then between the A's and the As a relation that we will call 'otherness' (= $a′$), a relation whose meaning is that the A's, although they present the generic character b of all Bs, are at the same time 'other' than the As or 'different' from them. The property of otherness is one which depends on A and on the property a characterising its elements.[18]

And here is the second possibility: at a further stage of development in infancy, the complementary class— that is, the storage room of what is different from A—becomes able to subsume every kind of things: hence, not only the birds that are not ducks but also all the objects that, in addition to not being ducks, are not even birds—for example, dogs, stars, colours, emotions. Piaget and Inhelder also write: 'The two types of negation which have a general meaning [. . .] are negation with respect to the whole (i.e. not-A in the absolute sense) and negation with respect to the next including class (which gives the secondary class A′, i.e. the Bs that are not-A).'[19]

---

18 Ibid., p. 129.
19 Ibid., p. 140.

These two forms of negation, connected with the more or less broad extension of the complementary class, correspond to successive stages of maturation of verbal thought.[20]

---

20 As a counterpoint to Piaget's investigations, we should bear in mind the remarks of a great and little-known linguist: Antoine Culioli. In his essay, 'La négation. Marqueurs et opérations' (in *Pour une linguistique de l'énonciation* [Paris: Ophrys, 1990]), he puts forward the idea that logical negation is the result of a 'primitive operation', probably rooted in ontogenesis, with which the speaker identifies and, at the same time, differentiates lexical notions. It is worth noting that the positive pole of the 'primitive operation', that is, the acknowledgement of stable semantic values, itself presupposes the cognition and examination of the different, the *héteron*. Culioli writes: 'By means of identification, the subject assumes that an occurrence *a* is an occurrence of the notion A [. . .] Without identification, we cannot construct terms, or relations between terms, or references' (ibid., p. 96). The exceptional importance of this procedure explains 'the privileged character of the positive term as the representative of a *lexis* that is neither positive nor negative but, rather, compatible with both the positive and the negative' (ibid., p. 97). That is, it explains the juxtaposition—already examined in the previous chapter—between the affirmative form and a sense that is as such always neutral, open in equal measure to assent and denial. And yet Culioli specifies that identification relies on the survey, and the ensuing cancellation, of the differences that subsist between the various instances of the same lemma: 'One takes on the responsibility for alterities that, however, are eliminated' (ibid.). We could therefore say that, even before giving rise to the complementary class A′, which includes all that which is not A, what is different participates in the establishment of the positive class A itself. 'In short, identification is the alterity taken into account and then eliminated; differentiation

In the course of ontogenesis, there first appears a different-from-x that still has characterizing properties. Presuming that the complementary class of non-ducks is nonetheless composed by birds, the child does not hesitate to attribute to it the entire host of affirmative predicates that is under the jurisdiction of this species: the non-duck is a winged animal, it has feathers and a beak, etc. Up to this point, the *héteron* is used above all for the construction of a hierarchical order among classes: A (ducks) + A′ (non-ducks) = B (birds); B (birds) + B′ (non-birds) = C (animals); C (animals) + C′ (non-animals) = D (living beings), etc. This is already a lot, but not enough. The advent of negation as such requires one more step: the institution of a complementary class, that is, of a different-from-x, that is exempt from any kind of positive connotation. How, precisely, is this further step accomplished? Far from being nourished by the original and rudimentary 'intuitive otherness', the formation of an undetermined *héteron* depends on the full development of the ascending hierarchy of classes. According to Piaget, there is a discovery that makes a real change, one that completes the system of complementarity: if class A (ducks) is less extended than class B (birds), and B is less extended than C (animals), etc., then the negative class not-A (that which is different from ducks) will be more extensive than not-B (that which is different from birds), and a fortiori than non-C (that which is different

---

is the preservation of alterity. Alterity is thus foundational' (ibid.). Logical negation and its explicit symbols are born out of the twofold movement by means of which difference is first occulted and then exhibited. After having negated the *héteron* in order to fix an identity, we again refer to negation, but this time in order to indicate the *héteron* that is opposed to the identity we have just obtained.

from animals), etc. The hierarchical relation between classes of increasing extension is reversed when we consider their complementary classes. The *héteron* of duck is the most comprehensive and less circumscribed, since it includes not only the non-duck birds but also non-birds, non-animals, non-living beings, etc. The statement '*x* is not a duck' now no longer entails the affirmation '*x* is a bird' but leaves the physiognomy of *x* entirely undecided. Negation becomes endogenous—that is, such that it concerns in principle any possible locution—when it refers to the complementary class that is hierarchically the highest, that is, to an unlimited and indefinable *héteron*. This *héteron* lacking any specifiable quality is a propitious resource for the child who is acquainting himself with the use of the 'not'; it is also the only one on which the *Sophist* dwells.

In Plato's dialogue, the question of complementary classes, of their genesis and extension, comes to the fore when the Stranger makes Theaetetus notice that 'The nature of the different appears to be parceled out.'[21] The *héteron* is subdivided into infinite parts, each of which is juxtaposed like a shadow to a particular positive meaning. The set of terms different from 'red' are opposed to it, and it hardly matters whether they belong to the field of colours: this set obviously includes 'blue' and 'green', but also 'strong', 'quick', 'prudent', etc. This all-embracing set, unified only by its complementarity to 'red', is the fraction of *héteron* that takes the name of 'not-red'.

> STRANGER. There exists a part of the different that
> is set in contrast to the beautiful?

---

21 Plato, *Sophist*, 257c7–8.

THEAETETUS. Yes.

STRANGER. Are we to say it is nameless, or has it a special name?

THEAETETUS. It has. Whenever we use the expression 'not beautiful', the thing we mean is precisely that which is different from the nature of the beautiful.

[. . .]

STRANGER. May we not say that the existence of the not-beautiful is constituted by *whatever* thing among other existing things [*állo ti ton ontón*] that is being marked off from a single definite kind and again set in contrast with something that exists?

THEAETETUS. Yes.[22]

The class of the 'not-beautiful' is bound in each of its aspects to the semantic content of 'beautiful'. It exclusively includes what, not sharing its properties, is other than 'beautiful'; but this other-than-beautiful, which never has a positive identity, is fully included, without any omission. Precisely because it lacks an autonomous definition, the complementary class 'not-beautiful' enjoys an indiscriminate extension. In the *Sophist*, 'given a certain class A, the expression "not-A" corresponds to a complementarity in relation to "everything" (i.e. to Z, which is the most general class of the system)' and not 'in relation to B, the class immediately larger'.[23]

---

22 Ibid., 257d–e (emphasis added).

23 Piaget and Inhelder, *The Early Growth of Logic in the Child*, p. 137.

The *héteron* guarantees the transition from a childhood-Parmenidean language, in which negation is resolved into a new affirmation ('Paolo is not beautiful' = 'Paolo is weird'), to a verbal thought endowed with all of its means, one that is able to negate a semantic content even if it deals only with it, and hence does not have to put forth an alternative content ('Paolo is not beautiful' does not have any theme other than Paolo's beauty). As a gap that cannot be sutured in the compact positivity of perceptive and sensorimotor experience, the *héteron* announces the independence of human discourse from environmental states of affairs and from emotional stimuli. The *héteron* is a threshold. And, like all thresholds, it has an *ambivalent* nature: it separates and connects at the same time; it marks an irreversible detachment, but marks it by radicalizing the defining traits of the situation from which it separates. The key here is to understand that the *héteron* documents a genesis; it does not present a conclusive balance sheet. But let us look more closely at what its ambivalence consists of.

It is certainly the case that the reference to the different as different, that is, to a complementary class that is so extended that it remains undetermined, blocks the introduction of any further meaning by the 'not'. However, it is no less the case that the category of difference, including in itself all the properties that could supplant the negated property, insistently evokes precisely that introduction of a further meaning which, on the other hand, it blocks. These two concomitant truths combine with each other: the category of difference evokes a possibility in order to block it or, even better, it blocks it only because it evokes it. Let me clarify. By saying 'Paolo is not beautiful,' I decide not to specify what predicate different from 'beautiful' suits 'Paolo', but I decide this because the *héteron* my negation refers to is so vast that it embraces the whole set of possible predicates. What inhibits the actual *replacement* of a meaning ('beautiful') with another particular meaning ('ugly' or 'weird' or 'intelligent', etc.) is precisely a *replace-ability* that, being unlimited, does not envisage any real-ization. In both the *Sophist* and infancy, negation acquires a full right of citizenship when the *héteron* no longer alludes to an individual semantic content but designates the *class* of all semantic contents that do not coincide with the one that is about to be discarded. The reference to the class, *and only to it*, prevents the reference to one of its specific members. Many commentators frown and reproach Plato for not having been able fully to grasp the salient prerogatives of negation: as a spokesman of what is different, negation would preserve an undue affirmative undertone. This is actually an embarrassing misinterpre-tation, one that is immediately dispelled if we adopt an ontogenetic standpoint in reading the dialogue. Both in ontogenesis and in the itinerary followed by the Stranger and Theaetetus, what precedes negation is not archived once and for all but persists as a residual aura in the way in which negation starts to operate. I repeat that the *héteron* is a threshold: in crossing it, we bid farewell to a form of thought that, however, is still impending. It would be inappropriate, and even farcical, to confuse this farewell, which is not without harshness, with a fervent declaration of fidelity.

4.4

BEING WHAT IS DIFFERENT, SAYING WHAT IS DIFFERENT[24]

In order to write a not-too-fictional biography of the *héteron*, it is worth patiently noting down the occurrences of the term in the *Sophist*. I mean the occurrences that are conceptually relevant, those that punctuate memorable episodes in the life of the protagonist. Here, their perusal is preceded by a rudimentary reflection whose only aim is to identify from the beginning a possible criterion of classification. It is also preceded by a succinct reconstruction of the parts of the dialogue where the *héteron* initially appears as a character.

What is different is one and double. We do not understand much about it if we overlook or exorcize the duality that characterizes it. On the one hand, the *héteron* belongs to the set of things expressed by language. It in fact amounts to the semantic loot of that peculiar discursive operation that is negation: 'non-courageous' means 'different from courageous'. On the other hand, the *héteron* is an unavoidable component of language in general. It weaves together the texture of all discourses and, before that, makes possible the very existence of the auditory or graphic organism we call 'discourse'. We already know that the relation between signs—on which the propositional format of human thought depends—is supported by their difference: it is only because they are *héteroi*, non-identical, that the signs 'Giacomo' and 'courageous' can be combined in the statement 'Giacomo is courageous.' As we will see later, this is only one example of the multiple ways in which the *héteron* determines the nature and

---

24 'Essere il diverso, dire il diverso'. [Trans.]

functioning of verbal activity. Although it also figures among the things that language *says*, what is different first of all pertains to what language *is*. Having to explain its vocation for double standards, handbooks get by with judicious disquisitions about the coexistence in the *Sophist* of an 'ontological level' and a 'linguistic level'. Reading them, it almost seems as if Plato dwelt for many pages on the heterogeneity of entities as entities, and only later inferred from this preliminary exploration some important corollaries concerning the status of negative statements. These are but cultural irritants. It is enough to skim the *Sophist* to realize that nothing is more linguistic than the so-called ontological level: in question there is precisely and only the *being of logos*. We can thus outline a criterion of classification of the occurrences of the term 'different'. They have to be divided into two big groups: (1) those that refer to something we do by speaking: *saying* what is different; (2) those that refer to the way in which our speech is made: *being* what is different. From a taxonomical point of view, what matters most is the distinction, but also the reciprocal reference, between the *héteron* expressed by negation and the *héteron* that contributes to forging any kind of expression.

Being what is different: this is a definition of language as a whole. Saying what is different: this is a particular linguistic act. In Plato's text, the explanation of how one can say what is different comes last. Thus, what comes last is those occurrences of the term *héteron* that concern negation[25] and the false.[26] At the beginning, precedence is given

---

25 See Plato, *Sophist*, 257b6–258b4.
26 See ibid., 262e6–263d4.

to what is different as a way of being. All the initial occurrences of the term *héteron* revolve around the hidden
structure of language or, if we prefer, around some requisites that make discourse what it is. Such occurrences
are placed in the long interlude in which—having by then
acknowledged the impossibility of giving a face to the
medanós on, the absolute non-being—the Stranger and
Theaetetus are searching for other ways to clarify the existence and deeds of the sophist. It is worth taking a closer
look at this juncture of the philosophical and ontogenetic
drama we are witnessing. In what situation does being-
what-is-different surface? And how do we extrapolate that
it fully corresponds, in all of its nuances, to the inner life
of language?

Having failed their first attempt at deciphering the
meaning of the syntagm 'that which is not' (*to me on*), the
Stranger and Theaetetus react by examining the meaning
of its apparent contrary, that is, 'that which is' (*to on*). For
Parmenides, but also for thought in infancy, only being is
sayable, and, consequently, only affirmative statements are
meaningful. Made cautious by the setback they have just
suffered, the two interlocutors do not move any prejudi-
cial objection to this belief, and content themselves with
testing it. How do we actually say being (a being in which
what is sayable would be exhausted)? And what is the
nature of affirmative statements (apparently, the only
legitimate ones)? To answer both questions at once, the
Stranger and Theaetetus examine four affirmative statements on being: (1) dualist philosophers claim that being
is composed of two fundamental parts; (2) monists claim
instead that being is one and indivisible; (3) the irascible

materialists—Plato calls them 'sons of the earth'—assert that being is the incessant movement of perceivable bodies; (4) finally, the 'friends of ideas' maintain that being pertains only to intelligible forms, not subject to movement and becoming. Now, none of these four statements turns out to be reliable. For a blatant reason: their characteristic agencies (dualism, monism, unconditional supremacy of movement, absolute primacy of rest) all involve in their own way the *abolition of verbal language*. Pay attention to the fact that this is the same abolition that was previously attained by the intention to seize the absolute non-being, the *medanós on* (see 4.2). The statements on being contain provisions that, were they satisfied, would ultimately exclude the possibility of enunciating. I will shortly show what these provisions are, in each individual case. For the time being, I limit myself to putting forward some intuitive remarks. The above hypotheses vanish as soon as they are formulated in words: in fact, their actual utterance provides for the refutation of the obstacle to uttering they nonetheless imply. It is moreover evident that being, the fatherland of the sayable, is always and at any rate safe from definitions that postulate the waning of saying in general.

The initial occurrences of the term 'different' go together with a survey of the contradictions that undermine the assertions on being. Let us turn to the reason for this concomitance. The various ways in which dualism, monism, materialism and idealism cause the catastrophe of logos evidence, by contrast, the requisites that logos must have in order to exist. These requisites, without which language could not function as it does, all revolve around the notion of *héteron*. At the end of the day, dualism, monism, materialism and idealism destroy articulated discourse because they suppress the relations of non-identity that constitute its framework. The term *héteron* emerges in Plato's text to right a wrong: in reactivating the relations of non-identity improvidently cancelled by the affirmations on the *on*, it gives back to language what was illicitly taken away from it. The *héteron* thus emerges where the conditions of possibility of speaking are at stake. Or, better: where the *discourse on being* is obligatorily turned into an enquiry into the *being of discourse*.

4.5
METAMORPHOSIS OF THE *HÉTERON*

My survey of the occurrences of '*héteron*' is organized as follows: first, I indicate the specific acceptation of the term to which we have to pay attention; I then follow on with a brief commentary that, at least in the first cases, signals the link between the emergence of that acceptation and the misadventures of one or other ontological statements discussed by the Stranger and Theaetetus. Occurrences (a), (b), (c), (d) and (e) concern what language *is* (being what is different). Occurrence (f) functions as a bridge between the *héteron* as a condition of discourse and the *héteron* as an object of discourse. Occurrences (g) and (h) account for the non-identities that language *expresses* (saying what is different). The locution 'different from' is entirely equivalent to the little word 'not' and can only be replaced by it. Equivalence and the possibility of replacement, which are as such unsurprising, nonetheless gain a singular theoretical relevance in the occurrences of '*héteron*' where the way of being of logos is at stake: in these it becomes clear that, well before carrying out a major role in describing the world, the syntactic connective 'not' already mirrors certain salient traits of verbal activity considered as a whole. That is, it becomes clear that negation, referring above all to the nature of the system-language of which it is part, has a decidedly *reflexive* origin. Let us put an end to these premises; here is the catalogue.

(a) *The grammatical subject is different from (is not) the predicate that is attributed to it.*

Dualist philosophers claim that 'Being is what is hot and what is cold.'[27] This assertion tacitly presupposes that the grammatical subject 'being' is identical with the predicate 'hot' and the predicate 'cold'. If this were not the case, we would need to count three distinct elements, not just two: in addition to hot and cold, being—which having its own autonomous meaning cannot be assimilated to them—should also be counted. However, those who grant the identity of subject and predicate run into another no-less-serious inconvenience. The two elements of which being is composed according to the initial hypothesis are fatally reduced to one: assuming that the predicate 'hot' and the predicate 'cold' both coincide with the grammatical subject 'being', one is forced to conclude that 'hot' and 'cold' are in turn one and the same thing. Dualism is refuted by its own enunciation. Furthermore, our generic capacity to enunciate, that is, the mere fact that we speak, is sufficient to dismantle dualism. If the subject were identical with the predicate, as dualism requires, we could not express anything by means of words: the affirmation 'Giacomo is courageous' would limit itself to communicating that

27 Ibid., 243d8ff.

'Giacomo is Giacomo' or, alternatively, that 'Courageous is courageous.' The dualistic hypothesis is indefensible because it abrogates an essential characteristic of verbal language. In order to form an articulate discourse, it is necessary that the grammatical subject is *héteron* with respect to the predicate, and hence that it is *not* the predicate. What is 'different', as a plausible double of non-being, safeguards predication, avoiding the equation of the latter with a judgement of identity, that is, with a tautology.

(b) *The predicate* x *is different from* (*is* not) *the predicates* y, z, w, *etc.*

What holds for the relation between grammatical subject and an individual predicate also holds for the relation between several predicates that are inherent to a single subject. Thus, this latter relation is itself negative-differential: when I say 'The cat is white and fast,' I imply that 'white' is *not* 'fast'. Multiple properties can be simultaneously ascribed to the same object or event only because they are different and irreducible to one other. The Stranger observes:

> When we speak of a man we give him many additional names—we attribute to him colors and shapes and sizes and defects and good qualities [. . .] we say he is not merely a 'man' but also 'good' and infinite other things [*hétera ápeira*]. And so with everything else. We take any given thing as one and yet speak of it as many and by many names.[28]

---

28 Ibid., 251a8–b4.

The non-identity of the various predicates is a fundamental condition of propositional thought. If language
were not intertwined with non-being, that is, with the
héteron, such a condition would not subsist. In that case,
Parmenides or the preschool child would certainly be
right in claiming that 'It is impossible that many things are
one and one is many.'[29]

(c) *The word is different from (is not) the thing for which it
stands*.

Monistic philosophers state: 'Being is one.' But this
hypothesis is contradicted by the distinction between
word and object—a distinction on which every discourse
is based, including the one that formulates the monist
hypothesis. If only 'one assumes that the name is different
[*héteron*] from the thing, one is surely speaking of two
things'.[30] Being is not one because the term that says it
is something different from its referent. To defend his
stance, the monist can only cancel the difference between
ónoma and *prágma*, sign and what is designated, meaning
and denotation—with regrettable consequences: 'If one
assumes that the name is the same as the thing, either one
will have to say it is not the name of anything, or if one
says it is the name of something, it will follow that the
name is merely a name of a name and of nothing else
whatsoever.'[31]

Sounds without semantic content or futile self-
references: this is what words become when we annul

---

29 Ibid., 251b8–9.
30 Ibid., 244d3–4.
31 Ibid., 244d6–9.

the gap that separates them from things. In his lessons on the *Sophist*, Heidegger writes:

> The *ónoma*, precisely as *ónoma*, as expression, is supposed to be an expression *of* something, [. . .] something that the *ónoma* is not, a *héteron* [. . .] If they wanted to identify the name with what is nominated, the expression and what is meant in it, made visible in it, then indeed the expression would be an expression of nothing.[32]

Like the dualistic position, the monistic one in turn implies the impossibility of speaking; hence it too is refuted by the fact that after all we do speak. More precisely: monism is refuted by the unquestionable discrepancy between signs and reality, without which there is no doubt our language would instantaneously vanish. Not being the object it nonetheless accounts for, maintaining a detachment with regard to what it shows: this is the irrevocable requisite of any saying. Exhibiting nothing less than the lasting non-identity between logos and being, the third occurrence of the *héteron* is perhaps the most important.

(d) *The* name (ónoma), *the vocal sign of rest, is different from* (*is* not) *the* verb (rhéma), *the vocal sign of movement. Discourse takes place only through the conjunction of these two* héteroi.

Materialists declare that 'Being is incessant movement.' The idealists reply that 'Being is absolute rest.' Both opinions are irreconcilable with knowledge, given that it requires at the same time determined—that is, static—concepts and dynamical inferences: 'If all things are

---

32 Heidegger, *Plato's 'Sophist'*, p. 313.

unchangeable, no intelligence can really exist anywhere in anything with regard to any object [. . .] On the other hand, if we allow that all things are moving and changing, on that view equally we shall be excluding intelligence from the class of real things.'[33]

It is only later, when the dialogue is about to end,[34] that Plato brings to light why the hypotheses of the 'sons of the earth' and of the 'friends of ideas' imply a deterioration of cognition. Both materialists and idealists eliminate the difference, and thus also the intertwining, between names (*ónomata*) and verbs (*rhémata*). A statement that is shaped by pure movement will only include vocal signs that indicate actions, that is, verbs. On the other hand, a statement complying with the perfect rest in which being would dwell can only use vocal signs that are names. The 'sons of the earth' reduce *ónomata* to *rhémata*; the 'friends of ideas' reduce *rhémata* to *ónomata*. Independently of the outcome, this reduction sabotages the construction of intelligible sentences, and thus inhibits knowledge: 'A statement never consists solely of names spoken in succession, nor yet of verbs apart from names.'[35] If they were coherent, materialists should resign themselves to saying 'walks runs sleeps': but 'that does not make a statement'.[36] Utterances such as 'lion stag horse' would suit the idealists that are ready to take their principles seriously: but 'such a string never makes up a

---

33 Plato, *Sophist*, 249b5–10.

34 See ibid., 261d1–262e7.

35 Ibid., 262a9–11.

36 Ibid., 262b7.

statement.'[37] The name is *not* a verb, and the verb is *different from* the name. In virtue of their heterogeneity, name and verb enter into a relation and form statements endowed with sense. In the previous occurrences, the *héteron* showed differences of semantic character. Here, on the other hand, it sanctions the non-identity of the syntactic functions that coexist within any discourse.

(e) *The logos is the power* [potenza] *of connecting* (dýnamis koinonías) *different elements.*

In order to avoid the dead-ends of the dualists, monists, 'sons of the earth', and 'friends of ideas', the Stranger proposes an autonomous definition of being, that is, of what is sayable, that, far from opposing the nature of logos, is finally in harmony with it, that is, with the conditions on which saying depends. While the ontological statements we have analysed so far are subjected to what is different as a sudden perturbation, or a fearful return of the repressed, the hypothesis advanced by the Stranger relies on it. Here is the hypothesis: being is 'power [*dýnamis*] either to affect anything else or to be affected'.[38] It goes without saying that entities have the power to act and be acted upon independently of what we say in their regard. This is clearly attested by the third occurrence of *héteron*: words are different from the things they designate. However, although being is not logos, it is only from logos— from its internal organization—that we obtain the notion of power we need to adequately define being. Language

---

37 Ibid., 262c1–2.
38 Ibid., 247e1.

is *dýnamis koinonías*,[39] the power of connecting heterogeneous elements: consonants, vowels, articles, names, etc.
Thanks to the *koinonía*, that is, the connection, each part
of discourse shows its ability to influence the other parts
and to be influenced by them, to act and being acted upon.
This prototype inspires the definition of being that Plato
opposes to traditional ontologies, which are all devoted
to the *impotentia loquendi*, that is, to an irremediable atrophy of speech. Logos is the power to put into relation: but
the relation requires that the correlates are different. The
koinonía, which guarantees the existence and the ability
to signify [*significatività*] of statements, is in turn guaranteed by the *me on*, by the non-being as *héteron*, that is, in
the end by the non-identity of the connected elements.
The subject *can* be united with the predicate because it is
not the predicate; predicate x *can* coexist with predicate y
because it is not predicate y; a word *can* refer to an object
because it is not that object; a name *can* combine with a
verb because it is not a verb.

The power of connecting different elements is also
the power of *not* connecting them, hence of keeping them
separate, conferring in this way a special relevance to their
difference. The *dýnamis koinonías*, which is the cornerstone of the logos, remains open to both positive and negative cases. After all, this applies to any *dýnamis*: the one
who is able to love is equally able not to love. Of course,
if nothing could mix with anything else, there would not
be even a trace of discourse.[40] But if everything could
indiscriminately mix with everything, discourse would

---

39 Ibid., 251e9 and ff.
40 See ibid., 251e8–252d1.

implode, because of phonetic malformations, syntactic inconsistencies, semantic indeterminateness.[41] A lack of *koinonía* or, on the contrary, a *koinonía* without limits: childhood monologues, the verbal documents of psycho-pathological disturbances, and many ritual formulas (since rituals re-evoke the anthropogenetic process, that is, the still-uncertain and partial formation of the characteristic traits of our species, in order to alleviate an individual or collective crisis) oscillate between these two poles. But in the ordinary language of the adult, the *dýnamis koinonías* is always selective and regulated. The *héteron* presents itself at the same time as a condition of the mixture and as what remains at each turn excluded from it. The words 'movement' and 'agile', precisely because they are differ-ent from each other, can be linked in the statement 'Andrea's movement is agile.' But if Andrea were a para-lytic, in spite of having the ability to be linked, 'move-ment' and 'agile' would not actually be linked. The *héteron* that comes to the fore as an effect of a failed *koinonía* is mostly expressed by a negation: 'Andrea's movement is *not* agile'. The power of connecting, as the other side of the power of not connecting, already anticipates—even though only in passing—the passage from what is different qua the permanent structure of logos to what is different qua that which the logos designates only occasionally. In short: the passage from non-being to the 'not'.

(f) *The* héteron, *which makes possible the connection between all words, is also a word connected with the others. It is a con-dition of possibility of the* léghein, *of saying; nonetheless, it*

---

41 See ibid., 252d2–10.

never fails to manifest itself as a circumscribed legómenon, *something that is said, a commonly used verbal expression.*

Wishing to understand more deeply the *dýnamis koinonías* of which language is made, the Stranger and Theaetetus decide to test the relation between some key words, called 'the greatest kinds' (*meghíste ghéne*). What are these kinds? Heidegger's advice seems to me irreproachable: when Plato writes *proelómenoi ton meghíston legómenon átta*,[42] we should not understand it as 'Let us choose some of the things that are said to be the greatest' but as 'Let us choose some of the greatest things among those that are said.' We are therefore facing 'a dialectical discussion of what is said most properly and primordially in every addressing of things as such'.[43] Although they have their own partic- ular meaning, the keywords the two interlocutors are dealing with are also the categories that allow us to under- stand how the meaning of discourses in general is formed.[44] The Stranger initially mentions three *meghíste ghéne*: 'being', 'movement' and 'rest'. In question is the way in which they mix, partake of one another and pred- icate one another. Let us suppose we say 'movement is' and 'rest is'. In assessing these statements, it is useful to recall the critique moved earlier to the dualists' hypothesis: if the predicate 'being' were not something different, or *héteron*, from 'movement' and 'rest', that is, from the grammatical subjects to which it belongs, then these sub- jects, being both indiscernible from the predicate they

---

42 Ibid., 254c4.

43 Heidegger, *Plato's 'Sophist'*, pp. 370–1.

44 John Lloyd Ackrill, *ΣΥΜΠΛΟΚΗ ΕΙΔΩΝ* in Gregory Vlastos (ed.), *Plato I: Metaphysics and Epistemology* (New York: Doubleday & Anchor, 1971[1955]), pp. 207–9.

share, would be identical. This is an absurd outcome: nobody can doubt that movement (*rhéma*, i.e. 'verb') differs from rest (*ónoma*, i.e. 'name'). The terms 'movement', 'rest' and 'being' are correlated and mixed because 'each one of them is different [*héteron*] from the other two, and the same [*tautón*] as itself.'[45] The list of keywords, of the *meghíste ghéne*, thus needs to be extended: 'But what do we mean by these words we have just used—"same" and "different"? Are they a pair of kinds distinct from those three, though always necessarily blending with them, so that we must consider the kinds as five in all, not three?'[46]

We now have under our noses the principal scene of the philosophical (and ontogenetic) play devised by Plato. Any investigation on the background of linguistic negation can benefit from it: even the investigation of those who, lamenting the *Sophist*'s insufficient familiarity with the theory of evolution, are awaiting inspiration from Stephen Pinker's forthcoming articles. What happens precisely in this episode of the dialogue? It is here that the *héteron* is split in two, or at least moves from a liquid to a solid state: the property that makes possible the mixing of all the *ghéne* is in turn condensed into an autonomous *ghénos*, distinct from the others. What is different is pervasive and localized: it is both a relation between words and an independent word; a presupposition of predication and an individual predicate; a constitutive principle of the logos and a particular product of the logos. In addition to providing information about the structure of any kind of enunciation, the crucial term figures as an explicit component of

---

45 Plato, *Sophist*, 254d14–15.
46 Ibid., 254e2–255a1.

certain statements: 'Movement is different from being,' 'Luigi is different from a loyal man,' etc. The *héteron* is located within that *koinonía* which, on the other hand, it enables and promotes; it is, at the same time, the rule and the ingredient of the interweaving of verbal signs out of which discourse arises. Occurrence (f) builds a bridge between *being* what is different and *saying* what is different. It marks the place where what language *is* is transformed into something that language *expresses*. It would be wrong, however, to overlook the bridge as such, that is, the nexus that links the two aspects. When I say what is different (e.g. by means of a negation: 'Andrea is not an ill-mannered person' can well stand in the place of 'Andrea is different from an ill-mannered person'), I treat it as a prominent *ghénos*, a term among others, a specific predicate; but the *ghénos* 'different' is only the condensed reflection of the differential relation between various *ghéne*, between the parts of discourse; in this way, the different that I happen to be *saying*—possibly using its twin 'not'—is always rooted in the different that diffusely characterizes the *being* of the logos.

The coexistence, as well as the partial juxtaposition, of what is different as a *condition* of discourse and what is different as an *object* of discourse fatally generates ambiguities, double meanings and logical circles. It even generates actual paradoxes. Qualifying the relation between all words, the *héteron* also qualifies the relation between itself, as a particular word (or *ghénos*), and the words with which it combines: 'Is motion different from difference [*héteron tou hetérou*], just as it was other than the same and other than rest?—Necessarily.'[47]

---

47 Ibid., 256c4–6.

The *héteron* is a category that applies to itself: there is no term that is not different from 'different', and, reciprocally, the term 'different' is and remains different from all others. The pervasive *héteron*, that is, the non-relational non-being that animates the logos considered in its totality, fully involves the localized *héteron*, that is, the lemma by which it is nonetheless designated. If we then try to unravel the relation of the 'different' with the specular *ghénos* 'identical', we end up in an entanglement analogous to the one delineated by the antinomy of the liar: what is different, if it is identical with itself, is then different; but if it is different from itself, then it is identical. I repeat that paradoxes arise when the same concept is, at the same time, a rule and a concrete case to which the rule applies, a condition of possibility and a phenomenon from which it derives, a relation and a correlated individual entity. I would add however that these paradoxes are virtuous, since they mirror with the greatest fidelity the coming and going between being what is different and saying what is different from whence negation originates. What is really circular is the nexus between the *héteron* that enables us to speak and the *héteron* expressed by speech, between the original non-identity of 'Paolo' and 'beautiful' and the empirical statement 'Paolo is *not* beautiful,' between the 'not' that accounts for the nature of language and the 'not' at work in a specific linguistic act.

(g) *'The negations "me" and "ou" as prefixes indicate something different from the words that follow'*.

On this point[48] I have already said everything I had to say (see 4.2 and 4.3). I do not think it is appropriate to propose

---

48 Ibid., 257c1–2.

again refrains such as 'Negation does not introduce a new semantic content, alternative to the one inherent to the corresponding affirmation;' or 'The *héteron* which negation initiates is always undetermined, devoid of positive attributes, not liable to descriptions,' etc. There is no point in re-examining this. Rather, it is worth paying attention to the context—slowly surfacing in the last few pages—in which we now need to inscribe our remarks. The portrayal of negation becomes clear and fitting, that is, reliable, only if we insert the occurrence of 'different' that directly concerns it—that is, occurrence (g)—within the entire sequence of occurrences of the same term. It is the sequence as a whole that shows the intimate solidarity between what is different as a way of being of language and what is different as that which at times language indicates by putting *me* and *ou* before other words. The *héteron* hinted at by a particular discourse through the syntactic connective 'not' is a metamorphosis, or a sort of reification, of the interstitial *héteron* that makes possible the existence of any discourse. The relations of non-identity that set up the logos (the subject is *not* the predicate; the word is *not* the thing it designates; the name is *not* the verb; etc.) lie at the foundation of logical negation ('Mario is *not* courageous'); and vice versa, logical negation symbolizes always and again those basic non-identities—it is their legitimate heir and most authoritative spokesperson. The 'not' projects onto a specific predicate, as part of a contingent proposition, the game of differences that constitutes the unavoidable structure of every predication and every proposition.

Although it is also related with the other occurrences of *héteron*, negation derives above all from two of the occurrences we have discussed. In the first place, it derives from occurrence (e): the logos is *dýnamis koinonías*, a power of connecting different elements. We know that this power also manifests itself negatively, as a deficit of connection, a blocking of the mixture, a permanent or temporary gap between certain meanings. The different that is excluded from the *koinonía* is precisely that which the logical operator 'not' aims at. In order to focus on the failed factual link between 'Socrates' and 'mad', or the essential incompatibility between 'movement' and 'motionless', we happen to say 'Socrates is *not* mad' and 'movement is *not* motionless.' Negation gives a linguistic appearance to the impossibility of connecting everything with everything in language. The limit of the *koinonía* is exhibited by the singular form of *koinonía* that a negative statement is. What is different, and as such participates in the formation of all discourses insofar as it is a *disjunction that correlates*, instead presents itself, both in the power of *not* connecting and in negation *sensu stricto*, as a *relation that disjoins*. The second, and more visible, introduction to the use of the 'not' can be found in occurrence (f): the 'different' is an independent *ghénos*, an autonomous meaning, a term that is really uttered. Negation bursts on the scene when the *héteron*, that is, the category that accounts for the internal organization of our speech, attains in turn the status of a word that is said, participating as a predicate in countless statements. The predicate 'is different from' has a functional equivalent in the locution 'is not': hence it is always possible to convert 'Renato is different from an ox' into 'Renato is not an ox.' The *semantic* content of the syntagm 'different from' is coagulated in the *syntactic* connective 'not' which is applicable in general to any semantic content. The two occurrences of *héteron* we have just recalled, (e) and (f), have much in common with the evolution of thought in infancy, and thus with ontogenesis. Both the power of *not* connecting the parts of a discourse and the individuation of what is different as an independent *ghénos* carry out an important task in the constitution of the complementary classes of undefined extension (all that is different from 'duck'; all that is not 'red'; etc.); according to Piaget, it is by referring to them that the child begins to master negation with increasing ease.

(h) *The false discourse, around which the form of life of the sophist revolves, amounts to saying 'things different from the things that are'.*[49]

The ultimate defence of the 'hundred-headed sophist' is along the following lines: a statement endowed with sense is always true, given that, in order to make sense, it must refer to something that is; those who want to say the false would speak about nothing, and hence would not speak at all, emitting only a series of meaningless sounds; if we concede that falsity is indistinguishable from the lack of sense, it is no longer legitimate to accuse sophists of producing false discourses, verbal images (*eidola legómena*) to which nothing corresponds; anyone can in fact verify that sophistic discourses abound with well-defined semantic contents. The Stranger crushes this argument by showing that the sense of a proposition has nothing in common with its truth-value: the words 'Riccardo limps' are comprehensible for anyone even before we ascertain whether we are using them to tell the truth. Meaning is neutral, open to both confirmation and denial. Its existence does not depend to any extent on the capacity to denote things

---

49 Ibid., 263b7.

as they are, but only on the *dýnamis koinonías*, the regulated and selective mixture of heterogeneous elements: 'Words which, when spoken in succession, signify something, do fit together, while those which mean nothing when they are strung together, do not.'[50]

The statement 'Theaetetus flies' can be considered to be false only because it *already* has a meaning [*senso*], as such consistent, that is the result only of differential relations between the parts that compose it: 'The sounds uttered do not signify [. . .] anything that exists or does not exist, until you combine verbs with names.'[51]

The coexistence of sense [*senso*] and falsity is confirmed in particular by occurrence (c) of the *héteron*: words are different from the things for which they stand. A proposition is really a proposition, and not a signal dictated by the events that follow each other in the surrounding environment, because the logos is *not* being; but, precisely because the logos is *not* being, the proposition is always able to depict 'things different from the things that are'.[52] The difference between the word and the object then sweeps through language, where it is presented as the difference between two functions the latter carries out: meaning [*significato*] is *not* denotation; sense [*senso*] is *not* truth-values. The gap that separates meaning from denotation institutes the empty space in which lies and errors creep in. The sophist inhabits this crack in the positivity of experience.

---

50 Ibid., 261d9–e2.

51 Ibid., 262c2–5.

52 Ibid., 263b7.

Negation and false discourse are ways in which we say what is different. One question that arises is whether the capacity to *say* what is different, achievable in these two ways, also invests the statements that concern *being* what is different. More to the point: Can we negate, or consider as false, the principles established by the first five occurrences of *héteron*? Can we negate, or consider as false, that 'the subject is different from the predicate', that 'predicate *x* is different from predicate *y*', that 'the word is different from the thing it designates', that 'the name is different from the verb', that 'the logos is the power of connecting different elements'? The answer is negative. We are subjected to a curious limitation: at the precise moment when I try to negate the statements in question, or to denounce their falsity, I fully confirm their content. For an evident reason: insofar as occurrences (a), (b), (c), (d) and (e) of 'different' define the very nature of discourse, when we dispute them discursively we always need to abide by the conditions they postulate, independently of our subversive intentions. When I say 'I reckon that it is *false* that the subject is different from the predicate,' or 'The logos is *not* a power of connecting different elements,' I can say it only because the subject is different from the predicate and the logos is a power of connecting different elements. It is well known that Aristotle supports the principle of non-contradiction,[53] that is, the necessary definiteness of verbal meanings, by observing what happens to the one who claims to refute its applicability: as long as he expresses himself with intelligible words, the aspiring refuter in fact already corroborates the point he refutes in the very act of refuting it. Something similar

---

53 Aristotle, *Metaphysics*, IV, 1006a, 12 ff.

happens in the case that interests us: the attempt to assert that the fundamental semantic and syntactic differences—without which no assertion could take place—are different from what they are is repudiated by its own implementation. We are not allowed to call into question the reality of the *me on*, the relational non-being that pervades our speech from top to bottom. What is radically *undeniable* is the constitutive negativity of language: the 'not', whose task would be to negate it, is in fact the legacy and the condensed projection of this negativity.

Our survey of the occurrences of the term 'different' in Plato's text comes to a close here. Now, as we are about to conclude, let us recall the problem that troubled the Stranger and Theaetetus at the beginning of the dialogue. How to explain the unquestionable yet apparently absurd existence of the sophist? What is responsible for a form of life characterized by a surprising confidence in unreality? I have already noticed that the sophist is less isolated and bizarre than he may seem. There are other human types who show an analogous competence in trafficking with non-being: the compulsive ironist, who never tires of suggesting what he thinks by declaring what he does *not* think; the opportunist, who entrusts his own affirmation to ephemeral possibilities, commendable precisely because they are only *eidola legómena*, verbal images that do *not* yet denote anything; the postmodern sceptic, inclined to renunciation, postponement, omission, and hence to a variety of negative actions through which one does *not* do something. It would not be difficult to add further examples. What matters is acknowledging that the Stranger and Theaetetus' search is virtually extended to the set of behaviours, habits, linguistic games and passions in which we can visibly recognize the 'factual existence of *me on* itself' (Heidegger). But let us return to the sophist. From the beginning, it is clear who he is: a man who 'expresses things that are not'.[54] It is not a matter of describing his activity, which everybody already knows, but of individuating the ground that nourishes it, that is, the conditions that make it possible. What is in a nutshell the outcome of the investigation?

Plato's dialogue proceeds like a spiral, as it traces increasingly wider circles around the same phenomenon. This phenomenon, both logical and ethical, is indeed the concrete form of life of the sophist. By saying what is false, he speaks of what is *not*. In order to understand how it is possible to say what is false, and hence how the sophist is possible, we need to shed light on negation, on the powers of the 'not' that animates the locution 'that which is *not*'. But in order to establish what negation is, it is necessary to go back to the rules and limits of predication, to the interweaving of the different syntactic functions and to the relation between words and things. Here is the key point: the conditions that make possible the activity of the sophist blatantly coincide with the way of being of the logos, with the internal structuring of statements and with the 'generative grammar' of human speech. As to avoid misunderstandings, let me promptly specify that what is in question is not the obvious weight that discourse has in all forms of life, but the development of a peculiar form of life that is directly embedded in the requisites without which a discourse would not be such. The praxis of the sophist follows closely the *me on*, the

---

54 Plato, *Sophist*, 240e1.

non-being qua *héteron*, which, according to Plato, is lodged in verbal language. We could say the same thing using Saussure's jargon: though all speakers have to come to terms with the 'complex of eternally negative differences' which make up language, only some speakers organize their existence in immediate and explicit harmony with this complex. Among these stand out the sophist, the compulsive ironist, the opportunist and the sceptic who renounces, postpones and omits.

4.6

NON-BEING ACCORDING TO HEIDEGGER: THE CENTRALITY OF MOODS

The relation or, better, the reciprocal reference between non-being and logical negation is the cornerstone of the *Sophist*. This very relation has a prominent place, albeit only as a polemical target, in *What Is Metaphysics?*—the inaugural speech Heidegger delivered at Freiburg in 1929 when he was offered the chair that had been Husserl's. To the best of my knowledge, *What Is Metaphysics?* is the only instance in the entirety of Heidegger's *oeuvre* in which he explicitly deals with the crucial theme of Plato's dialogue from an autonomous theoretical stance. There are other texts in which Heidegger reflects on the Nothing or, alternatively, on negative assertions and the status of the 'not', but it is only here that the two aspects are examined together, and what is involved is their interweaving and friction. Everything points in the direction of the fact that the 1929 speech is the continuation and the actual conclusion of the course on the *Sophist* Heidegger taught

at Marburg in 1925.[55] However, this continuation and conclusion marks a clear break with the speculative kernel of
the work he commented line by line some years earlier.

In order to grasp at once, at least broadly speaking,
the reason for this break, we have to recall how carefully
Heidegger evidenced, in his university course of 1925, the
existential dimension of Plato's enquiry into negation and
false discourse: the life of the sophist is the 'factual existence of *me on* itself'; the Nothing is embodied in the
works and days of a particular human type. Now, in *What
Is Metaphysics?*, Heidegger has come to the conclusion that
the 'factual existence of *me on* itself' is too serious an issue
to remain bound to an examination of linguistic practice.
The ways in which the Nothing infiltrates the existence
of all of us (hence, not only that of the sophist) do not
share much with the capacity to say that which is *not*.

---

55 There is copious textual evidence that corroborates this
hypothesis. Let us consider only one example. The passages of
What Is Metaphysics? in which Heidegger establishes how difficult it is to speak of Nothing seem to be a very close paraphrases
of the perplexities that torment the Stranger and Theaetetus
when they start their *tour de force*: 'What is the nothing? Our
very first approach to this question has something unusual
about it. In our asking we posit the nothing in advance as something that "is" such and such; we posit it as a being. But that is
exactly what it is distinguished from. Interrogating the nothing—
asking what and how it, the nothing, is—turns what is interrogated into its opposite. The question deprives itself of its own
object. Accordingly, every answer to this question is also impossible from the start. For it necessarily assumes the form: the
nothing "is" this or that. With regard to the nothing question
and answer alike are inherently absurd' (Heidegger, *What Is
Metaphysics?*, p. 85).

Given that logic never manages to seize the Nothing, the latter will have to be accounted for by referring to a repertoire of pre-logical experiences which are far more basic than the concepts—already aimed at a semantic and syntactic analysis—employed by the Stranger and Theaetetus. However strange this may seem, Heidegger distances himself from the setting of the *Sophist* only to endorse its most conspicuous result: the discovery of a form of life that is shaped by non-being. This singular mixture of distance and proximity is very useful to understand—independently from Heidegger and in open contrast with the hypothesis he promotes—which problems should be taken charge of by a theory inclined to clarify the *anthropological* range of linguistic negation, that is, the eminent role that the syntactic connective 'not' plays in the material and sentimental vicissitudes of our species.

For Plato, non-being and negation are united by the category of the *héteron*, which is the cornerstone of both. As a synonym of 'non-being', the *héteron* is one with the nature of language considered as a whole. As a counterpart of the 'not', the *héteron* is rather something that language says at times. The double function attributed to the 'different', which is obviously a strong point of the *Sophist*, authorizes us to think that negation transforms the ubiquitous and unapparent non-being that weaves the texture of the logos into a considerable expressive resource. In *What Is Metaphysics?*, Heidegger separates the two poles that the polysemy of the *héteron* joined and made commensurable. This separation first takes the shape of a misleading hierarchical supremacy of one pole over the other: 'Is the nothing given only because the "not," i.e. negation, is given? Or is it the other way around? Are negation and the "not" given only because the nothing is given? [. . .] We assert that the nothing is more original than the "not" and negation.'[56]

But the real demarcation does not at all lie in the precedence of the non-being with respect to the sign 'not'. Plato himself takes for granted that the *me on* is 'more original' than negative statements. And yet, according to Plato, this *me on*, which without doubt precedes any circumscribed locution, corresponds to the pure and simple existence of language. On the other hand, for Heidegger, the Nothing is 'more original' than negation because it inhabits the *non-linguistic* relation that the human animal has with the world, that is, with the 'totality of beings'. Radically heterogeneous from verbal thought, the Heideggerian *me on* mostly manifests itself in certain characteristic *moods*. Among them, anxiety is especially important—a feeling of fear and disorientation that, spreading rapidly without having an empirical trigger, signals our permanent maladjustment to the environment. Heidegger writes: 'In anxiety, we say, "one feels uncanny" [. . .] We cannot say what it is before which one feels uncanny. As a whole it is so for one. All things and we ourselves sink into indifference. [. . .] Anxiety reveals the nothing.'[57]

We thus need to recognize the 'factual existence of *me on* itself' in the individual who falls prey to an anxiety resistant to words, and not in the loquacious author of negative propositions.

---

56 Ibid., p. 86.
57 Ibid., p. 88.

Simplifying, the alternative is therefore the following: on the one hand, a Nothing that is indistinguishable from the way in which our speech is made; on the other, a Nothing strongly linked to the non-linguistic experience of the world as a vital context that is partly undetermined and unpredictable. The first kind of non-being finds a miniaturized alter ego in negation; the second is announced by anxiety and by other emotional moods (for instance, boredom). Heidegger's great merit is having stressed the centrality of feelings and affects when the Nothing is at play (of course, provided that we consider feelings and affects as the most reliable index of some salient traits of the human condition, and not as 'a transitory epiphenomenon of our thinking and willing behavior'[58]). But the centrality of emotional moods does not in any way imply that the Nothing, which they bear witness to, is unbound from verbal language. What should prevent us from supposing that these moods issue from the *me on* inherent to our speech? Where is it written that 'emotional' should necessarily rhyme with 'pre-linguistic'? The Platonic non-being, that is, the *héteron* that shapes the structure of all discourses, is never emotionally inert: to think otherwise would be an intellectual catastrophe. When we repeat the reassuring adage that man is 'the animal that has language', *zoón lógon échon*, we all too often overlook the emotional dimension of the 'has', that is, of the *échon*. The possession of a biological organ characterized by a 'complex of eternally negative differences' by itself generates specific moods. What matter here are not the statements that convey one or other passion but those

---

58 Ibid., p. 87.

passions correlated with the mere capacity of enunciation. It is precisely this capacity that causes always and again the disorientation that Heidegger calls 'anxiety'. Those who prefer a magniloquent and allusive vocabulary may well say that anxiety reveals the Nothing, but they should also be sensible enough to add that the Nothing revealed by anxiety is embedded in *having* language, in the *échon* that is wrongly deemed to be only an ancillary component of the syntagm *zoón lógon échon*.

The fact that the feeling of anxiety originates in the negative experience of logos is, after all, also suggested by a cautious, or at least not hypnotized, reading of *What Is Metaphysics*? The characteristics Heidegger assigns to the anxiety-inducing Nothing essentially match those presented by the 'that which is not' in the *Sophist*. In both cases, what is extracted from the horizon of the investigation is absolute non-being, the *medanós on*, in other words, the collapse of any conceivable reality. Heidegger writes: 'Beings are not annihilated by anxiety [. . .] The nothing makes itself known with beings and in beings [. . .] The nothing does not remain the indeterminate opposite of beings but reveals itself as belonging to the Being of beings.'[59]

Like the Platonic *héteron*, the Nothing supported by Heidegger is itself inseparable from being, and even fully permeates it. How is the 'totality of beings', that is, the environment in which we live, presented in the light of anxiety? This feeling signals a *detachment* from objects and events: it makes us 'shrink back'[60] from them; it draws

59 Ibid., p. 90, p. 94.
60 Ibid., p. 90.

them away into a sort of vanishing point; it makes them alien to us. But without this detachment, which the Nothing institutes and anxiety at times displays, we would not be able to grasp objects and events for what they are, and distinguish them from our psychological representations: 'In this very receding things turn toward us.'[61] At the end of his lecture, Heidegger affirms that the detachment from the environment enables us to enter into a relation with 'Being as such'.[62] The locution 'as' (*als*), at first sight humble and pleonastic, is the most appropriate correspondent of the Nothing: we therefore have to think that, by revealing the Nothing, the emotional mood of anxiety also gives great prominence to the 'as'. Let us ask on what conditions we can understand a being *as* such, that is, maintaining a distance from it. The intuitive answer is: on condition of *saying it*. I depict the thunder *as* such because the word 'thunder' is *not* the thing it stands for; because the predicate 'dangerous', with which I qualify it, is *different* from the grammatical subject 'thunder'; because I speak of the thunder thanks to a proposition, that is, a *koinonia* of elements regulated by negative-differential relations; because I am always able to *negate* that there is thunder or that it has a certain aspect; because I may say something *false* about it. The Nothing, which determines the detachment from the environment, is indiscernible from the 'as', but the 'as' is in turn indiscernible from the life of language. The anxiety-inducing disorientation, which 'leaves us hanging' and often 'robs us of speech',[63]

---

61 Ibid., p. 88.

62 Ibid., p. 95.

63 Ibid., pp. 88–9.

is the emotional face of the Nothing that is connatural to the very fact of *having* the logos.

In the previous chapter (see 3.2 and 3.4) I insisted on the distinction between two types of negation: the *onto-logical* one, which mirrors the way of being of our dis-courses, and the *empirical* one, whose task is disconnecting a specific predicate from a specific subject ('Mario is not happy,' 'The war is not lost,' etc.). Ontological negation ratifies the fractures that dominate any statement or, better, the fractures without which a statement would not be a statement: sense is *not* denotation; sense is *not* the illocutionary force; sense is *not* something present. As the first and most decisive reference of the sign 'not', these infra-linguistic caesurae are perhaps akin to the occur-rences of the *héteron* that set the conditions of possibility for verbal language. Like the capacity to *say* what is different in the Platonic dialogue, empirical negation consists of projecting onto the state of affairs of which we are speaking the original negativity that thrives in speech in general. The distinction between two types of negation allows us to solve once and for all the issue dear to Heidegger: the role carried out by certain emotional moods, anxiety in particular, in making us aware of the Nothing.

Ontological negation attests to the *neutrality* of lin-guistic sense, that is, its independence from environmental states of affairs and psychic drives. Given that environmen-tal states of affairs and psychic drives determine the pres-ent, we could also say that, being independent from both, sense always enjoys a considerable *untimeliness*. The neu-trality and untimeliness of the semantic contents that are expressed at each turn involve a systematic *detachment* of

the speaker from the 'totality of beings'. Ontological negation, which is the driving force and guarantor of such a
detachment, gives rise to a variegated congeries of feelings.
These are feelings that emerge in the gap between sense
and denotation, sense and illocutionary force, and sense
and presence. They are, indeed, feelings of detachment.
The independence of linguistic activity from environmental states of affairs and psychic drives carves out a no-man's
land where we find both remorse and the Shakespearian
desire to 'tread on kings', both paralysing hesitation and
the longing for the unforeseen, both marvel and cynicism.
What about anxiety? I will refrain from elaborating upon
my doubts regarding the actual consistency of this passion
and, above all, the presumed impossibility of deriving it
from more elementary emotions.[64] Let us continue for a
moment to play Heidegger's game. If it is something,
anxiety is the mood that originates from a heightened
relation with ontological negation, a stupefied contem-
plation of the heterogeneity between logos and being, and
an abnormal dilation of the voids and pauses caused by
the untimeliness of sense. In anxiety, ontological negation
is transformed into an existential attitude: 'Sense is *not*
something present' becomes 'We are suspended before
being as it dissolves in its totality.'

It is easy to observe the (not only lexical) affinity
between the disorientation (*Unheimlichkeit*) brought about
by anxiety and the feeling of the uncanny (*das Unheimliche*)
studied by Freud. As we all know, the uncanny is something familiar, by which we previously felt protected and

---

64 See Virno, *E così via, all'infinito*, pp. 63–9.

reassured, that now suddenly resurfaces with a disquieting or even threatening face. The doppelgänger, this double that now upsets us, is the sinister counterpart of the immortal soul to which the primitive man entrusted his survival.[65] Similarly, the 'totality of beings', within which we felt until recently at ease, is transfigured by anxiety into something alien and distant. Anxiety-inducing disorientation is the horrific doppelgänger of the habitual exchanges we have with the things and facts of the world: the confidence with being *as* such, on which these exchanges rely, is turned into the excruciating impression of never being at home. What is less well known, but far more important, is the divergence between these two emotional moods. On close inspection, they delineate opposite and specular reactions to the negativity of logos.

While anxiety disproportionally stresses the detachment from the environment, the uncanny decrees a temporary abrogation of this detachment, thus validating a frightening symbiosis between representations and represented things. Freud writes that it is a matter of 'a regression to a time when the ego had not yet marked itself off sharply from the external world and from other people. [. . .] An uncanny effect is often and easily produced when the distinction between imagination and reality is effaced [. . .] when *a symbol takes over the full functions of the thing it symbolizes.*'[66]

---

65 See Sigmund Freud, 'The Uncanny' in James Strachey (ed.), *The Standard Edition of the Complete Psychological Works of Sigmund Freud, Volume 17* (London: Vintage, 2001[1919]), pp. 234–6.

66 Ibid., p. 236, p. 244 (emphasis added).

The familiar-uncanny therefore celebrates its glory when words appear to blend with the objects for which they stand; when the *héteron* that keeps statements and facts separated is eclipsed; when the sign, being wholly juxtaposed to what it designates, abruptly ceases to be a sign. The uncanny obscures for a short period of time ontological negation—the very negation whose effects are instead exasperated by the feeling of anxiety. Those who fall prey to the Freudian *Unheimliche* taste the identity, only apparent but terrible and disorienting, between sense and denotation, sense and illocutionary force, sense and presence. While the mood of anxiety is the climax of the autonomy of the symbol with respect to what is symbolized, the feeling of the uncanny brings us back for a moment to the threshold between symbolic and pre-symbolic life: a threshold that can be attained only by the animal which, although familiar with symbols, is nonetheless always in relation to being *as* such. The detachment from environmental states of affairs and psychic drives produced by ontological negation is also and perhaps especially attested to by its intermittent (and pathological) repressions. Anxiety and the uncanny are the two polar versions—one paroxysmal, the other defective—of the same fundamental experience which never lacks an affective gradient: the experience of *having* language.

In *What Is Metaphysics?*, Heidegger divides the existential Nothing from logical negation, and vehemently opposes the 'factual existence of *me on* itself' to the powers of the syntactic connective 'not'. This splitting has a very high price, which we should refuse to pay. On the one hand, the *logical basis of the Nothing* is disregarded, that is, the latter's taking roots in the fundamental prerogatives of the logos; on the other, the *existential value of negation*, or—which amounts to the same—the effects of syntax on emotions, remain in the shadow. According to Heidegger, the 'not' would only be the breathless echo, or the miserable notary, of a series of non-verbal events, which would be vivid and moving: 'Unyielding antagonism and stinging rebuke have a more abysmal source than the measured negation of thought. Galling failure and merciless prohibition require some deeper answer. Bitter privation is more burdensome.'[67]

But is it really the case that antagonism, rebuke, prohibition, and privation are immune to the 'not'? What if instead they presupposed it and were shaped by it to different degrees? Heidegger's explanation about the possibility of formulating negative statements by means of a kind of pre-linguistic inclination to negate[68] can be countered with an exasperated remark Wittgenstein makes: 'How can the word "not" negate? Do we even have a concept of negation other than negation with a sign? Yes, we can think of something like: impediment, rejecting gesture, exclusion. But all of them as well are always *embodied* in a sign.'[69]

The impediment, the rejecting gesture, and the exclusion of which Wittgenstein speaks have much in common with the emotional situations mentioned by Heidegger: antagonism, rebuke, prohibition, etc. But

---

67 Heidegger, *What Is Metaphysics?*, pp. 92–3.
68 See ibid., p. 92.
69 Wittgenstein, *The Big Typescript*, p. 966 (emphasis added).

unlike Heidegger, Wittgenstein is sufficiently lucid to acknowledge that, apart from what the functioning of the sign 'not' teaches us, we do not have any notion of negation, or of non-being, and hence we do not even have notions of negative actions or passions. The 'not' is the *embodiment* (or, if we prefer Heidegger's jargon, the 'factual existence') of antagonisms, rejections, prohibitions and exclusions that are properly human.

5.
Negation and Affects

5.1
NATURAL HISTORY

'Commanding, questioning, recounting, chatting, are as much a part of our natural history as walking, drinking, eating, playing.' It goes without saying that both lists outlined by Wittgenstein in this passage of *Philosophical Investigations*[1] are partial, only indicative and may be extended at will. The first list, which focuses on things we do with words (and which we could not do otherwise), no doubt also includes describing events, praying, swearing, elaborating hypotheses, promising, forgiving, making

---

[1] Ludwig Wittgenstein, *Philosophical Investigations* (Oxford: Blackwell, 1953), p. 25.

jokes. To the second list, dedicated to behaviours resistant to words, we should at least add the avoidance of pain and the search for pleasure, empathy and aggressiveness towards our counterparts, the making of tools. However, what is truly interesting is not establishing with precision the virtual extension of the lists but recovering the nexus that connects them and causes their permanent cross-breeding. Reading the sentence from *Philosophical Investigations* we have just quoted, we soon wonder how the two kinds of activities combine; the former are linguistic, the latter non-linguistic, but they both partake, simultaneously and as equals, in defining the human form of life. What is the point of intersection between syntax and drives, statements and silent gestures, commanding and eating? The answer is unconditional: the intersection is realized by negation. Although it is located in the innermost and most disembodied area of verbal thought, negation relates the latter as a whole to sensorial and emotional experience. The 'natural history' of which Wittgenstein speaks has its cornerstone in a symbol, the 'not', that guarantees the articulation between symbolic universe and pre-symbolic vital conducts, relentless political conflicts and original harmony with the members of our species as an effect of mirror neurons.

Negation is not the late product of perceptual disappointment; it seems to me bizarre to suppose that it is forged by the surprise and irritation that overwhelm us when we suddenly realize that the splendid baroque building towards which we are walking is nothing but the cardboard backdrop of a cinematographic set. Neither can negation be passed off as the well-mannered emissary of passions that are too vulgar to appear in society, such as hatred and rancour. Nor is it the offspring of unsatisfied desires, the last metamorphosis of the mocking laughter the person we had begged for love reserved us. However, this does not mean that the syntactic connective 'not' is not continuously applied to every kind of perception, passion and desire, radically changing their texture and development. Although they do not at all depend on statements, hunger and fear take a completely different aspect as soon as they introject that distinctive trait of statements that is negation. Vice versa, because it is not a corollary or offspring of hunger and fear, negation has the power to transform their manifestations wholly or in part.

Earlier (see 3.3), I deplored the mistake made by those who carelessly confuse the *retroaction* of the 'not' on perception and affects with the perceptual or affective *genesis* of the 'not'. I now feel obliged to add that it would be an equally pernicious error to overlook or downplay the importance of retroaction, remaining satisfied with having clarified (or believing to have clarified) the traits of the genesis. We know that negation is the watershed that separates the sense of a proposition from psychological representations and inclinations. But this watershed is also the authentic bridge between semantics and psychology—not because of its implausible eclipse or attenuation but, on the contrary, for the same reasons that ensure its role as watershed. The following pages are concerned with showing how and why the logical tool that determines the discontinuity between linguistic praxis and drives nonetheless serve as the key with which the former intervenes in the latter, altering their fate. All in all, I intend to show how and why maximum separation paves the way for a lasting interweaving.

In the previous chapter, I claimed that the philosophical justification of negative statements—as undertaken by Plato in the *Sophist*—faces the same difficulties encountered by a preschool child when he accesses the use of these statements. It is perhaps worth reformulating the hypothesis that is particularly dear to me, namely, that of a retroaction of the 'not' on emotions and pre-linguistic behaviours, in light of Plato's dialogue and of the stage of development in infancy that stands as its ontogenetic counterpoint.

The initial obstacle the Stranger and Theaetetus run into in their attempt to defend the possibility of speaking of non-being is the arrogance with which the sophist equates discourses (*legómena*) with images (*eidola*). The image is always the image of something, and it cannot portray a lacuna or an absence, hence its nature is exclusively affirmative. Later on in the dialogue it becomes clear that verbal language is closely related to non-being, and regularly benefits from negation, precisely because it can never be reduced to the iconic dimension. But the heterogeneity of words from images, far from implying a drastic separation, favours their interpenetration. As the investigation is coming to a close, having ascertained the function that negation carries out in discourse and thus also in thought (*diánoia*) and opinion (*dóxa*), the Stranger and Theaetetus briefly discuss the nature of imagination (*phantasía*). This is the passage[2] to which I would now like to draw attention. Imagination is a 'blend of perception

2 Plato, *Sophist*, 264a8–b3.

and opinion' (*súmmexis aisthéseos kai dóxes*), where 'blend'
should be understood in the guise of the interaction of
hydrogen and oxygen that generates water, not in that of
the indifferent coexistence of water and oil in the same
bowl. Given that opinion is a linguistic construct (as the
'conclusion', *apoteleútesis*, of the 'dialogue of the mind
with itself' that is thought), *phantasía* amounts to the privileged place where words and sensible images are not only
linked but also united. In *phantasía,* words gain a sensual
physiognomy; their auditory body becomes an integral
part of a perception or an emotional state. However, it is
thanks to *phantasía* that the 'not'—an exclusive prerogative of discourses—enters into a territory, that of images,
which did not anticipate it. Consequently, the Stranger
concludes that imagination makes it possible for icons to
be themselves subjected to the rigour of negation—while
the sophist referred to them in order to ban negation.
Once mixed with the verbal signs of which opinion is
composed, images themselves *say* something; therefore
they too can be affirmed or negated, judged true or false.[3]
Whether we know it or not, when we speak of *phantasía*
we always speak of the way in which the syntactic connective 'not' retroacts on sensations, affects and desires.

The vicissitudes that punctuate the evolution of speech
in infancy are analogous. We have seen that it is marked
for a long period by a 'systematic disequilibrium favouring
affirmations'.[4] This disequilibrium, that is, the blockage
that inhibits negative statements, is due to the hegemony
exerted by perceptual and sensorimotor experience over

---

3 See ibid., 264 9–267d2.

4 Piaget, *Recherches sur la contradiction*, II, p. 164.

verbal utterances. The impossibility of negating images that emerge from perceptions and movements flows into discourses, conditioning the very construction of sentences: rather than observing that 'The flower is not red,' the child prefers to compose a new affirmation, with which he assigns the flower the quality of being yellow or purple. But what happens when the speaker begins to familiarize himself with the use of 'not'? The perceptual and sensorimotor images are in turn infected by the grammatical structures of the language that they themselves had previously infected. The capacity to say how things are *not* has repercussions in the field of experience that up to that point had curbed it. As the result of a by-now-bidirectional contagion between sensations and words, these repercussions are the inaugural act of strictly human *phantasia*. A decisive stage in the acquisition of negation by the child is the formation of complementary classes—for example, of a class that includes in itself everything that differs from 'red', without however specifying the hypothetical positive attributes that belong to this something that is different, that is, to the 'not red'. Now, it is a matter of understanding what shape childhood passions and actions take when each of them is juxtaposed with, and opposed by, a complementary class: non-rage (rather than an alternative feeling, e.g. amiability) for rage; the sheer omission of a gesture (rather than a further specific gesture y) for gesture x. The blending of statements with perceptions and drives, named *phantasia* by Plato, extends to perceptions and drives the *suspension without substitution* that characterizes from the outset the statements in which the 'not' appears.

5.2

A TWOFOLD INTERFACE

The term 'interface' designates the apparatus that, at the same time, separates and connects non-homogeneous systems or non-homogeneous phases of the same system. In information technology, we call interface the programme that makes digital and analogical calculators compatible. In physical chemistry, this name refers instead to the surface that registers the differences of intermolecular forces between the liquid and solid state of one and the same non-decomposable process. After these obvious examples, let me suggest a rather unpleasant one: the hard-nosed manager who confronts the insubordination of workers on behalf of his company does not fail to boast about his role as interface. But let us keep to the basics; the interface is both the *threshold* between different types or levels of reality and the *commutator* able to harmonize, and at times crossbreed, their specific properties. If this is the meaning of the term, we can then say without hesitation that negation is an interface. We can actually say that it fulfills such a delicate role twice.

Let us see on which occasions it does so.

(1) The 'not' is an interface because it is located at the crossroads between the way in which our speech is made in general and certain specific things that we do when we speak. On the one hand, it mirrors the 'complex of eternally negative relations' that permeates the inner life of language; on the other, it animates the particular statements with which we disconnect a predicate from a grammatical subject. In Platonic jargon, the 'not' connects the *héteron* as a condition of possibility of discourse (sense is

not denotation; the name is *not* the thing for which it stands, etc.) and the *héteron* as a contingent object of discourse ('Achilles was *not* a loyal fighter'). Negation works as a threshold, but also as a commutator, between two phases of a unitary system: one pervasive and coincident with what language *is*; the other condensed and circumscribed to something that language *expresses*. Here, it is easy to glimpse some similarities with the notion of interface in physical chemistry.

(2) The 'not' separates the pre-linguistic drives from verbal thought, and, at the same time, links them. It is the interface that determines the congruence and interweaving between the two lists of activities outlined by Wittgenstein: on the one hand, eating, drinking, walking, playing; on the other, commanding, questioning, recounting, chatting. In this case, negation is a border area where heterogeneous systems contaminate one another; this is not too different from the interface-programmes of information technology.

Acknowledging that the 'not' works twice, once as a threshold and once as a commutator, is nevertheless insufficient. What really matters is the articulation between the two instances. *Negation is an interface according to sense (2) because and only because it is an interface according to sense (1).* In other words, negation enables the retroaction of statements on emotions and on instinctual behaviours only because it translates into a concrete discursive operation that detachment from the environment and that gap from the present that characterize language considered as a whole. Having converted the negativity inherent to the very nature of our speech into a peculiar expressive resource, the 'not' is then applied to moods and affects; but, by virtue of this application, moods and affects are introduced into that basic negativity of which the 'not' is the specialized spokesperson. If they are subjected to negation, the pre-linguistic drives achieve a certain independence from the situations that should unchain them; they cease to adhere unconditionally to the 'now' and are liable to inhibition and postponement. The permanent untimeliness of linguistic sense, attested to and guaranteed by the syntactic connective 'not', also impacts emotions every time the 'not' is aimed at them. And the 'not' aims at emotions in the open laboratory of *phantasia* and of the imagination.

I would like to emphasize the paradoxical, or at least surprising aspect of all this. We know that negation has a *reflexive* vocation: although it is a specific element of linguistic signification, it participates in defining nothing less than the *meaning of the word 'meaning'*. Rather than enriching the description of the world, the 'not' deals exclusively with the relation that language entertains with the world. This is the reason why many authors have unhesitatingly claimed, with brutal oversimplification, that negative statements are meta-linguistic, or at any rate of a logical level higher than that of affirmative statements (see 2.6 and 3.7). Now, the paradox is the following: what modifies the physiognomy of our passions and desires are not signs endowed with a circumscribed meaning, possibly pertinent to emotional life (as is the case with 'sadness', 'longing', 'enjoyment', etc.), but the reflexive sign that fixes the meaning of 'meaning'. Sympathy, jealousy and concupiscence are not reshaped by words in general but by the syntactic connective that condenses in itself what makes a word what it is; not by particular linguistic products but by the *money of language*. In promoting the blending of sensations and discourses, *phantasía* privileges the component of discourses that offers an abbreviated yet perspicuous portrayal of the faculty of speech. Indifferent to statements about facts, the work of imagination rather avails itself of the logical device—negation—that evidences the *non*-identity between statements and facts. In short, language retroacts on the most elementary drives when it reflexively shows its way of being, and not when it gives vent to its denotative power [*potenza*].

In order to summarize the twofold manner in which negation carries out the typical duties of an interface, I will propose a rather simple schema. The vertical arrow, which unites the first 'not' to the second, indicates the dependence of interface (2) on interface (1). This is basically the symbol of an implication—the graphic equivalent of the canonical formula 'if . . . then'.

A		A1
What language *is* (untimeliness of sense, its detachment from the environment, etc.)	→ **NOT** → interface (1): meaning of 'meaning'	Something that language *expresses* (negative statements: 'The sea is *not* stormy,' 'I do *not* want to see you,' etc.)
	↓	
B		**B1**
Pre-verbal feelings and behaviours (desire, fear, shame, aggression, etc.)	→ **NOT** → interface (2): *phantasía*	Emotional life reshaped by syntax (emancipation of the drives from specific triggering causes; their possible inhibition, etc.)

5.3
A NEW EXPERIENCE OF PAIN

It remains to be seen *how*, with the help of negation, passions introject the detachment from environmental situations that, on top of being a requisite of every linguistic meaning, even qualifies the meaning of the word 'meaning'. To this end, it is worth examining a very common and unavoidable passion: pain. What we will say about it is also valid for a great number of other affects and moods: hostility, shame, distrust, etc. Relying on the schema I presented above, our theme is the metamorphosis pain undergoes in passing from column B to column B1; this passage is administered by the 'not' as interface (2). To illustrate this metamorphosis, I again draw on a passage by Wittgenstein, warning, however, that I am not here interested in providing an exegesis or commentary: 'A child hurts itself and cries; the grown-ups talk to it and teach it exclamations and, later, sentences. They teach the child *new pain behavior.*'[5]

The crucial question is the following: In what precisely consists the 'new behavior' evoked by Wittgenstein, that is, a way of living pain that is radically different from the one dominating the period when the child was not yet familiar with words?

It seems to me implausible that the experience of a passion is transformed in its entirety only because we learn to communicate it linguistically. Of course, the terms and sentences suggested by adults *replace* the inarticulate cry, which was a simple symptom of the perceived

---

5 Wittgenstein, *Philosophical Investigations*, p. 244 (emphasis added).

suffering. But as such this replacement does not inaugurate a 'new pain behavior'. The verbal expression that takes the place of a grimace or a lament can in fact be their functional equivalent. This is what happens in the case of affirmative statements in the first person: 'I have a pain' and 'I am in pain' are nothing but *signals*, like laments and grimaces. Statements of this kind do not yet constitute a distinction with respect to the pre-linguistic way of living a sensation or affect. Those who utter them often limit themselves to a *non-verbal use of verbal language*; that is, they employ words as gestural reactions. Replacing a certain signal (e.g. a shattering cry) with another signal (the exclamation 'I am in pain!') is significant from several points of view, but it does not explain anything about the reorganization of the drives accomplished by linguistic activity. It looks as though the 'new pain behavior' is developed only when the sentences in the first person cease to be the functional equivalent of a signal and start to transmit a meaning unbound to a specific cause or to some present circumstance. But how is a signal converted into a meaning? Or, using Peirce's jargon,[6] on what conditions does an *index* (the knocks on the door that announce a visitor) become a *symbol* (the semantic content 'arrival of a visitor', autonomous from any concomitant clue, and as such usable even if nobody will ever visit us)?

The answer is intuitive. A different lived experience of pain takes shape when the child—to whom the adults taught exclamations and later propositions appropriate to what he is feeling—discovers that he is able to utter the

---

6 See Charles Sanders Peirce, *Collected Papers* (Cambridge, MA: Harvard University Press, 1931–58).

negative statement 'I am *not* in pain.' We should recall that this discovery goes hand in hand with the formation of the complementary class 'different from pain'. The negative statement releases the affirmative one from the *status* of mere signal, *retroactively* granting it the consistency and prerogatives of a verbal meaning. It is only when we are able to say 'I am not in pain' that the sentence 'I am in pain' is separated from the cry which it replaces, rather than remaining its functional equivalent. By means of the 'not', we speak of pain even if we are not afflicted by it, and hence independently of what is *now* happening to us. But what makes a semantic content (sticking to the subject at hand: 'having a toothache') something inassimilable to a trace in the woods or a knock on the door is, indeed, its constant detachment from actuality. Negation turns a signal into a meaning (i.e. an index into a symbol) precisely because, exhibiting the caesura between discourses and facts, it contributes to forge the very meaning of 'meaning'.

The negative statement paves the way for *dissimulation*; the suffering child sometimes states 'I am not in pain,' fearing that confessing how he feels would prevent him from participating in games or an excursion. But the capacity to dissimulate a passion always implies the opposite and specular capacity to *simulate* it. When we know how to negate what is, we also know how to affirm what is not. According to the *Sophist*, these are the two connected ways in which we say the *héteron*, the different. The 'new pain behavior' thus includes the possibility of staging stoical denials and exhibitionist fictions. The expertise in dissimulating and simulating takes all innocence away from the wild exclamation 'I am in pain!' In other words, what vanishes is the impression that, at least in this case, the sense of the statement is identical to denotation. When we sincerely proclaim our pain, we nonetheless always take into account that, using the same words, we will in the future act the part of the victim, or that, introducing a minuscule 'not', we could have disavowed a fact that is for us evident. Wittgenstein[7] ironically observes that if the infant and the dog do not simulate, this is not because of their superior honesty but because they do not have access to the experience of pain that is made possible only by language. To be more precise, we should say: the infant and the dog do not simulate because they do not have negation at their disposal. Or, also: because they ignore that 'blend of perception and opinion' of which the imagination of *Homo sapiens* is made.

Let us reconsider the modus operandi of *phantasia* in light of these last thoughts. It connects the immediate perception of pain with the semantic content of the statement 'I am in pain.' But 'I am in pain' becomes a semantic content, and thus emancipates itself from the original role of signal, only after we have learnt how to say 'I am not in pain.' Having acquired a certain confidence with the 'not', the child notices the distance that also separates 'I am in pain' from the state of affairs he is living. This distance, exhibited by every authentic meaning, is the breeding ground of *opinions*. As soon as it stands out against the background of its possible negation, the affirmation 'I am in pain' brings with it a set of implicit conjectures concerning the nature and seriousness of the illness ('I'm

---

7 Wittgenstein, *Philosophical Investigations*, pp. 249–50.

fucked,' 'It's nothing'), the necessary cures, the measures that would have prevented it, etc. And it is precisely these conjectural opinions, inserted in the permanent detachment of meanings from facts, that *phantasía* mixes with the sensations we fall prey to. The imaginary mixture of passion and discourse, ultimately founded on the faculty of negation, generates the 'new pain behavior'. The suffering of the linguistic animal is therefore always and in any case *fantastic* [*fantasiosa*].[8]

The statements we are dealing with are all *in the first person*: 'I am in pain,' 'I hate him,' 'I am hungry,' etc. With regard to negation, what distinguishes them from statements in the third person, for example, 'The sea is stormy,' or 'Socrates is just'? The latter express a public sense that has nothing in common with the psychological

---

8 Wittgenstein (ibid., p. 246) claims that it would be nonsensical to say 'I *know* I am feeling pain.' The grammar of the verb 'to know' in fact implies the possibility of doubt and error: there is no knowledge that is not confronted with the alternative true / false. It is only the others who *know* that I am in pain, since it is only them who can mistake my state. On the other hand, I do not doubt the suffering that I am inflicted, I never ask myself whether it is true or false. That is why I do not *know* that I am in pain but simply *have* it. Wittgenstein's argument is too sketchy to be convincing. Each time I decide to dissimulate my suffering with the negative statement 'I am *not* in pain,' I adopt to a certain extent the point of view of those who are asking themselves about how I feel (so much so that I try to mislead them). Thanks to negation, the actor becomes at the same time a spectator, developing a cognitive, that is, conjectural and imaginative, attitude towards his own feeling. Certainly, I *have* pain, but since I hide it (or at least I am *able* to hide it) with the little word 'not', I also *know* that I have it.

representations of an individual mind; in Frege's words, this is a sense 'without a bearer'. Vice versa, the statements in the first person refer to the feelings and desires of that particular subject, or 'bearer', who is the author of a discourse. In the two cases, the 'not' carries out partially different functions. The statements in the third person are comprehensible for anybody to the specific extent that they can be negated; I would not understand the affirmative proposition 'The sea is stormy' were I not aware from the outset that the sense 'storminess of the sea' on which it revolves, being independent from facts (or better, from denotation), is also open to the negative proposition 'The sea is *not* stormy.' Things change when we say 'I am in pain' or 'I hate him.' Given that they verbalize the psychological representations of a 'bearer', the affirmative statements in the first person resemble signals. And the comprehension of a signal is realized without having to presuppose the possibility of negating it (after all, this possibility does not exist, since what contrasts a clue or a trace is only a new clue or a new trace, and never the syntactic connective 'not'). Unlike 'The sea is stormy' and 'Socrates is just,' 'I am in pain' and 'I hate him' are not meanings that are always deniable but *signals that become meanings only on condition that they are negated*. When what is at stake are feelings and desires expressed with words by those who feel them, negation *institutes* the semanticity of sentences, rather than figuring as the inevitable requisite of a semanticity that is already guaranteed from the outset.

In reorganizing emotional experience, the 'not' reorganizes linguistic experience itself or, better, that important part of it in which the signal seems to prevail over meaning and symbols are mostly used as indexes. In other words, the 'not' retroacts on passions on condition of first retro-acting on the verbal activity that is closer to the individual representations of a specific 'bearer'. Or, rather, on condition of tracing a clear borderline between the first person singular that characterizes the statements 'I am in pain' and 'I hate him' and the psychological subject who is in pain and hates.

The 'bearer' of perceptions, volitions and moods becomes a grammatical 'I' as soon as he is able to disavow what he nonetheless feels, asserting for example 'I am not in pain' or 'I do not hate him.' The first person speaks of the representations of which it would be the 'bearer', but speaking about them instantaneously stops it from being their 'bearer', since it can always drive them away by using negation. A passion from which we are able to distance ourselves, removing it or neutralizing it with the 'not', is to a large extent a passion that differs from the one condensed in the mental (and as such undeniable) images, or pictures, that punctuate our psychic processes. But different does not mean mitigated, assuaged or, worse, hypocritical. On the contrary, pain and hatred, when dissimulated or in any case distanced from the first person who speaks about them, reach an otherwise unconceivable intensity. Obviously, negated (or at least deniable) pain does not disappear but, separating itself from the particular circumstances that have caused it, often gives rise to the feeling of our enduring, and hence irredeemable, vulnerability. Negated (or at least deniable) hatred grows larger, acquiring a sort of 'free value', that is, a surprising autonomy from empirical events and circumscribed causes; it is no longer rage triggered by the actions of a certain individual but a total aversion for the very existence of that individual, independently of the particular actions he carries out. The first person nourishes passions that are more complex (because they are worked through by *phantasía*) and more radical than the ones ascribable to the 'bearer' of pre-linguistic representations. Freeing the grammatical 'I' from the limits of the psychological subject, the faculty of negation is fully responsible for this enhanced complexity and radicalism of our emotional life.

5.4
FREUD AS A THEORIST OF NEGATION

Freud's essay 'Negation' (1925) describes the way in which verbal thought is grafted onto affects, revolutionizing their dynamics. Its theme is the retroaction of syntax on drives. In spite of what is suggested by the legends nourished by the psychoanalytic tradition, Freud is interested in how language deforms psychic life, not in the psychological foundation of linguistic activity. More than delving into the functioning of the unconscious thanks to the examination of a strange use of negation, he evidences some prerogatives that pertain to negation *in general*, taking his cue from what he had already verified concerning the unconscious. It is indeed the case that Freud focuses on a borderline case: the revelation of an affect that had been repressed through the intervention of the 'not'. But the borderline case is strictly linked to ordinary cases ('I am not in pain,' 'I do not hate him,' etc.); it illuminates them and is illuminated by them in turn. The difference between the borderline case and the ordinary cases is quantitative. In short, it seems to me legitimate to propose a meticulous comparison, made more of affinities than contrasts, between the 'new pain behavior' hinted at by Wittgenstein and the discursive circumvention of repression to which Freud's reflections are devoted. This unusual comparison helps us to clarify how and why negation constitutes the authentic interface between meanings and desires.

It is known that Freud was impressed by the negative statements with which people undergoing psychoanalytic therapy—but also all other speakers, as can be ascertained by examining a casual conversation—betray an unconscious emotional tendency at the very moment when they disavow it. More precisely, he was impressed by the fact that this emotional tendency transpires only on condition of being verbally disavowed.

> The manner in which our patients bring forward their associations during the work of analysis gives us an opportunity for making some important observations. 'Now you'll think I mean to say something insulting, but really I've no such intention.' We realize that this is a rejection, by projection, of an idea that has just come up. Or: 'You ask who this person in the dream can be. It's *not* my mother.' We emend this to: 'So it *is* his mother.' In our interpretation, we take the liberty of disregarding the negation and of picking up the subject-matter alone of the association. It is as though the patient had said: 'It's true that my mother came into my mind as I thought of this person, but I don't feel inclined to let the association count.' [. . .] Thus the content of a repressed image or idea can make its way into consciousness,

> on condition that it is *negated*. Negation is a way
> of taking cognizance of what is repressed;
> indeed, it is already a lifting [*Aufhebung*] of the
> repression, though not, of course, an acceptance
> of what is repressed.[9]

When the psychoanalyst engaged in interpretation takes 'the liberty of disregarding the negation and of picking up the subject-matter alone of the association' (or, better, the pure *semantic* content of the statement with which the patient accounts for his psychic processes), he does not do anything special but behaves like any other animal endowed with language. Any speaker who runs across a 'not' regularly benefits from the 'liberty' claimed by Freud. On close inspection, it is not even a 'liberty' but an obligatory procedure. If an accomplice tells the robber Luigi 'I do not see any policeman at the entrance of the bank' and a patient tells Freud 'The woman in the dream is not my mother,' Luigi and Freud come to terms with the words they are hearing only if they identify the verbal thought, that is, the sense, that the negative statement shares with the corresponding affirmative statement: 'Seeing policeman at the entrance of the bank' in one case, 'Relation between the woman in the dream and my mother' in the other. Stating 'that not p' and stating 'that p' are two linguistic acts associated by the presence of 'p'. Leaving aside for a moment the 'not' at work in 'not p', the robber and the psychoanalyst grasp 'the subject-matter alone of the association', that is, the still undecided 'p', suspended between alternative developments. The meanings 'seeing policeman at the entrance of the bank' and 'relation between the woman in the dream and my mother'

---

9 Freud, 'Negation', pp. 235–6.

are as such neutral barometers, on which both positive and negative marks may appear. Availing themselves of their shared linguistic competence, Freud and Luigi move from the individual mark back to the barometer that makes it intelligible. We saw earlier (3.4 and 3.5) that the neutral sense '*p*', insofar as it is equidistant from the assertions 'that *p*' and 'that not *p*', fully manifests itself in the question '*p*?', or in the guise of the modal statement 'it is possible that *p*'. Listening to the patient who declares 'the woman in the dream is not my mother,' the psychoanalyst limits himself to explicitly formulating the question underlying that statement, the question in which its pure semantic content is condensed: 'Is the woman in the dream my mother?' The psychoanalyst notices that the question is also open to an affirmative answer.

There is much to be learnt from reading Sigmund Freud's 'Negation' (1925) while keeping an eye on Gottlob Frege's 'Negation' (1918–19). On some issues of crucial importance, there is a surprising and instructive convergence between these two homonymous texts, which have never been compared by the ventriloquist-interpreters of the two authors. As we will recall (see 3.4), for Frege, negating the sense of a statement does not amount in any way to the 'dissolution of its components'. If it were realizable, the destruction of a semantic content through negation would imply the conflagration of the sentence that expresses it, its dismemberment into unrelated fragments. But nothing of that sort happens: 'What we do is to insert the word "not", and, apart from this, leave the word-order unaltered. The original wording can still be recognized.'[10]

---

10 Frege, 'Negation', p. 123.

Freud can easily put into brackets the negation proffered by his patient precisely because, as Frege maintains, we all grasp the sense of a statement without taking into account the judgement of assent or dissent that accompanies it. The revelation of a repressed desire thanks to the discourse with which we repudiate it would not take place if negation did not faithfully preserve what it nonetheless suppresses. The 'not' deactivates the attribution of the predicate y ('is my mother') to the grammatical subject x ('the woman in the dream'), but in order to achieve this it still needs to exhibit it and present its possibility. If 'the content of a repressed image or idea can make its way into consciousness, on condition that it is *negated*,' it is only because negation, on the basis of its logical status, is obliged to openly speak about what it rejects. Psychoanalytic interpretation simply employs for therapeutic aims Frege's postulate according to which in every negative statement 'the original wording can still be recognized.'

However, it is evident that in the cases discussed by Freud the use of the 'not' distances itself in some aspects from the conventional model. The patient who promptly specifies 'the woman in the dream is not my mother' does not *presuppose* the semantic content 'relation between the woman in the dream and my mother', but *coins* it anew. He does not presuppose it for a simple reason: this semantic content concerns a desire that, having been up to that point unconscious, is totally ignored by him. The link dreamt woman / mother, which is at the basis of both a hypothetical admission and a hypothetical refusal, is instituted only by its refusal. The final outcome, that is, the negative statement, creates its own antecedent, that is, neutral sense. What is conditioned generates the condition on which it seems to depend. But there is more to it: in producing the semantic content on which it intervenes, negation also gives rise to the (until-then-unknown) psychic drive designated by the semantic content. That is, it shows for the first time the emotional state that constitutes the *extra-linguistic referent* of that semantic content. In addition to sense, the negative statement also forges denotation. For the subject as 'bearer' of psychological representations, the repressed affect, which by definition cannot be represented, is almost inexistent. This affect begins to exist only for the 'I' as the author of a discourse, for the grammatical first person that is able to keep it at distance by inserting a 'not' ('that is not what I intend'). In 'Remarks on the Function of Language in Freudian Theory', Benveniste summarizes the irruption of a hidden drive into the world of appearances as follows:

> Negation is in some way constitutive of the denied content [. . .] What then survives of the repression is only a repugnance to be identified with this content, but the subject no longer has power over the existence of this content. Here again, his discourse can produce denials in abundance but it cannot abolish the fundamental property of language, which is to imply that something corresponds to what is uttered, something and not 'nothing'.[11]

11 Émile Benveniste, 'Remarks on the Function of Language in Freudian Theory' in *Problems in General Linguistics* (Miami, FL: University of Miami Press, 1971[1956]), p. 73.

To clarify: it is as if, by saying 'I do not hate Gaetano,' the hatred for Gaetano that was 'nothing' became 'some thing', and only at that point—facing the 'some thing' brought to light by its negation—I started to feel the muscular contractions, the gnashing of teeth and the disgust that are the pre-verbal, either physical or psychological, manifestations of hatred.

We can now glimpse both the affinity and the divergence between the dissimulation of pain and the repudiation of an unconscious feeling. Let us start with the affinity. In both 'the woman in the dream is not my mother' and 'I am not in pain,' negation institutes the semantic content to which it applies. That is, it generates the neutral sense 'being in pain', which, unlike non-linguistic signs (laments, grimaces, etc.), preserves a pronounced independence from factual circumstances and from the present. In this way, a general law is outlined: each time it targets an affect, whether evident or repressed, the 'not' creates the meaning that befits it, rather than having it already at its disposal as an obvious premise. It is only negation that gives a semantic aspect to our emotional life. But here is the divergence. When we say 'I am not in pain' we at least presuppose the feeling of pain: a feeling that is present and pressing, if we use the 'not' to dissimulate it; a feeling that is however familiar, that is, experienced on other occasions, when the 'not' truthfully registers that, presently, we are unharmed by it. Here, the negative statement avails itself of a well-defined extra-linguistic referent: a passion firmly identified by perception or memory. On the other hand, as we remarked earlier, in 'the woman in the dream is not my mother,' negation makes appear for the first time a drive about which the speaker previously knew nothing. Freud's patient, like the child who asserts that he is not feeling pain after a massive fall, is to be considered a dissimulator; and yet, in the case of Freud's patient, *it is dissimulation that fully determines the physiognomy of the dissimulated affect.* I suffer from a pain even if I do not speak about it, but I notice an unconscious inclination to attack a close friend only when I reject it with the 'not'. To sum up: in the statement 'I am not in pain,' negation transforms an *already emerged passion* into a meaning; in the statement, 'the woman in the dream is not my mother,' negation *gives rise to* a desire while—and only because—it coins its meaning.

We are confronted with two specular possibilities. We may remove linguistically a known and even unquestionable emotion, endowed with its unmistakable somatic and psychological manifestations: 'I am not in pain,' 'I do not hate him,' 'I do not fancy her,' etc. But, thanks to the syntactic connective 'not', we may also linguistically reveal a repressed affective tendency: 'The woman in the dream is not my mother,' 'I do not intend to offend you,' etc. Both possibilities are embedded in the very nature of linguistic negation, that is, in the fact that 'it can annul only what has been uttered, which it has to set up for the express purpose of suppressing.'[12] In repressing with words a passion of which we are aware—for example, pain—what matters is the *suppression* of something that has nonetheless been formulated (and thus preserved). In revealing by means of words a drive that we do not want to acknowledge— for example the intention to offend—what matters is

12 Ibid.

rather the *formulation* (i.e. the exhibition) of something that is nonetheless repressed. The 'not' enables us to conceal a manifest feeling and to manifest a concealed feeling because it introduces a detachment with respect to the actuality of psychic processes, that is, because it disconnects the sense of our discourse from the 'now' in which perception and repression are settled.

Freud has no doubts: far from being bound to drives and desires, negation is actually the requisite that guarantees verbal thought a wide margin of autonomy with regard to them. Suffice it to quote some symptomatic passages:

> We can see how in this the intellectual function is *separated* from the affective process [. . .] With the help of the symbol of negation, thinking *frees itself* from the restrictions of repression [. . .] The performance of the function of judgment is not made possible until the creation of the symbol of negation has endowed thinking with a first measure of *freedom* [. . .] from the compulsion of the pleasure principle.[13]

'Separation', 'freedom'—such terms seem to me unequivocal. Claiming that the 'not' is a weak echo of our psychological disgusts, as lazy Freudians are fond of saying, is the opposite of what Freud puts forward. However, we should not believe that, since it does not derive from the passions, negation keeps at distance from them, and behaves dispassionately. On the contrary, it never fails to influence profoundly that affective process from which it is separated

13 Freud, 'Negation', p. 236, p. 239 (emphases added).

(or freed). All in all, it never fails to retroact on the drives and desires, modifying both their inclination and trajectory. The 'new pain behavior' evoked by Wittgenstein in *Philosophical Investigations* issues from the capacity to say 'I am not in pain.' Analogously, the negative statement 'the woman in the dream is not my mother' inaugurates a *new behaviour of the repressed affect*.

What does a repressed feeling turn into when it is brought to light by the words with which we reject it? Freud observes that negation 'is a way of taking cognizance of what is repressed [. . .] though not, of course, an acceptance of what is repressed'.[14] We keep on refusing a feeling that we now know we harbour. Rather than opposing and cancelling each other, this knowledge and this refusal are mutually sustaining: I know my intention to offend precisely because I refuse it; I refuse such an intention precisely because I know it. Both knowledge and non-acceptance realize themselves in the negative statement 'I have no intention to offend.' The neutral sense of this statement ('having intention to offend') is an object of knowledge; the 'not' is an instrument of non-acceptance. It is incorrect to explain the persistence of refusal even in the presence of knowledge by means of the ineptitude of the linguistic intellect to influence emotions. Better, this is incorrect in two ways. One does not realize that the couple knowledge/refusal, considered as a whole, exists only thanks to the logical operation of negation. And, above all, one does not realize that the indissoluble interweaving of knowledge and refusal delineates a new emotional constellation.

---

14 Ibid., pp. 235–6.

Being at the same time known and unaccepted, the feeling that has eluded repression is overwhelmed with ambivalence. The intention to offend to which I succumb is both familiar and alien. Or, better, it is familiar as still alien, and alien as still familiar; it is fully mine if and only if it is never really mine. Adopting the vocabulary of Plato's *Sophist*, we could characterize the affective experience that incorporates the use of the 'not' as follows: as soon as it is clearly expressed in order to repudiate it, the previously censored feeling no longer constitutes an absolute non-being, an unthinkable and unsayable *medanós on*, but a *héteron*, something different from emotions that we are prepared to admit, an impertinent predicate that is nonetheless endowed with sense. On condition of specifying that, in this case, the *héteron* does not concern what the 'I' says, but what the 'I' is. Refusing the emotional state that he nevertheless knows he is feeling, the author of the enunciation seems doomed to *not be what he is*, or, if we prefer, to be different from what he agrees to be. While the repressed drive was enfolded in the psychological subject, the feeling that surfaces linguistically, and is linguistically rejected, does not ever fully adhere to the grammatical first person. At times, this permanent non-adherence gives rise to *guilt*: I know well the passion that I nevertheless conceal. Or it foments *bad faith*: I conceal the passion that is nonetheless well known to me. But given that the knowledge of what is unacceptable is inseparable from the non-acceptability of what is known, we have to suppose that guilt and bad faith are themselves in agreement, often concomitant, and in some cases even interchangeable. Moreover, because it does not adhere to the 'I' that speaks, the known-and-refused feeling can take variable shapes. If it is formulated and suppressed in the same sentence, the intention to offend is no longer a disarticulated tendency but is unfolded in an indefinite plurality of dissimilar behaviours: cautious diffidence, or heedless rancour, or bored aplomb, or ironical excess of kindness, etc. The unconscious drive, as such shapeless, becomes truly *polymorphous* only when it is subjected to negation.

5·5
CONTAINING DESTRUCTION

I have repeated several times, like a broken record, that linguistic negation fully diverges from physical oppositions and from psychological contrasts. It is less absurd to strive to demonstrate the commensurability of the length and diameter of a circumference than to relate the functioning of the 'not' to disappointment, homicide, escape or vomit. And yet, in our concrete emotional experiences, the neat discontinuity of a negative statement with respect to various species of pre-verbal annulment does not manifest itself clearly. Especially in the case of the child who is acquainting himself with it, but also in that of an adult speaker who masters it, the act of negation seems at times a duplicate, or a faded reflection, of the material abrogation of some states of affairs. Although it is incontrovertible on a conceptual level, the heterogeneity between the use of the 'not' and physical struggle acquires visibility and weight only when it asserts itself in praxis, transforming to a certain extent our vital conducts. In order to show the gap that separates it from non-linguistic destructivity, negation can only enter in open conflict with the latter. The fact that the 'not' is something different from the hatred for an enemy and from the demolition of a defeated city is only attested by the possible application of the 'not' to hatred and demolition (i.e. it is attested by the statements 'I will not hate my enemy,' 'I will not demolish the city'). Denial is not a simple appendix to sad passions; this becomes evident only in the cases in which denial defuses or contains these passions. In order to modify feelings as a whole, negation first needs to paralyse, deviate or sabotage negative feelings. That is, it needs to refuse a refusal, expel an expulsion or cancel a cancellation. The alternative ways of annulling behaviours and matters of fact do not coexist in a regime of reciprocal indifference but clash brutally, like in a civil war. Their logical irreconcilability, so often unperceived, is practically (and emotionally) ratified by the salient episodes of this war.

I will limit myself to providing some examples of the procedures with which the 'not' intervenes on non-linguistic negativity, crushing or reforming it. These examples are not necessarily the most adequate. But this is of little concern—we will have to understand them as the rather casual beginning of an open list, which can be subject to any sort of extension and variation. By force of habit, the first two examples are taken from the essay by Freud on which I have dwelt in the previous section. Namely, the capacity negation has to abrogate that form of psychological abrogation that is repression; how and why negative statements contrast, or at least slow down, our inclination to expel from us what does not satisfy the pleasure principle. I add an almost superfluous warning: I will treat both issues with an eye on the anthropological range of negation, not in order to reconstruct and critically assess these Freudian hypotheses. The third example, which I draw from Nicole Loraux's investigations on Ancient Greece, concerns the public oath with which Athenians committed themselves *not* to remember the suffering they had been inflected during the aristocratic tyranny: a speech act that entrusted to the 'not' the task of blocking a foreseeable succession of retaliations.

(a) Repression, which is responsible for the banning of an affect, seems to have much in common with negation. It is its imperfect doppelganger or less developed ancestor. Freud writes: 'To negate something in a judgement is, at bottom, to say: "This is something which I should prefer to repress." A negative judgement is the intellectual substitute for repression; its "no" is the hall-mark of repression, a certificate of origin—like, let us say, "Made in Germany".'[15]

But shortly after he adds: 'With the help of the symbol of negation, thinking frees itself from the restrictions of repression and enriches itself with the material that is indispensable for its proper functioning.'[16]

The initial convergence is thus resolved into a separation. Although it resembles repression in some ways, the 'not' is the instrument with which we emancipate ourselves from the latter, and even remove it: 'Negation [. . .] is already a lifting of repression'.[17] The resemblance is evident: if the 'not' brings with it a detachment from the

---

15 Freud, 'Negation', p. 236.
16 Ibid.
17 Ibid., pp. 235–6.

actuality of perceptions and feelings, repression does the same, given that it distracts the subject from what he feels, confining the drives that nevertheless dominate him to non-presence. However, it is equally evident that there is a gap between the two phenomena: repression accurately cancels the psychic content from which it distances us, thus preventing its representation and even mention; on the other hand, negation preserves that which it suppresses, exhibiting the characteristic traits of the feeling it disowns. What is decisive by any standard is the way in which the second form of refusal, the one hinging on the 'not', weakens and finally overthrows the first. When it is applied to repression, negation causes a detachment from a previous detachment; it linguistically distracts from unconscious distraction; it renders untimely the non-verbal apparatus that sanctioned the untimeliness of an emotional tendency. Coquetting with Hegelian dialectic, we could speak of a *'repression' of repression*, or better, of a *negation of 'negation'*.[18] But the inverted commas I have added to one or the other term indicate that what is here at stake is the conflicting relation between two radically heterogeneous types of annulment of what is. One of the great merits of Freud's essay lies in suggesting that negation exercises its power in the field of affects only if it first sabotages and inhibits what resembles it the most, that is, the various kinds of pre-linguistic negativity. As I said earlier, negating repression is only an example of the systematic showdown between semantic destruction and psychological destruction.

---

18 See André Green, *Le travail du negatif* (Paris: Les Éditions de Minuit, 1993), pp. 43–72.

(b) According to Freud, one of the functions of judgement consists in 'affirm[ing] or disaffirm[ing] the possession by a thing of a particular attribute'.[19] Affirmation and negation have their apparent precursors in certain elementary drives:

> The attribute to be decided about may originally have been good or bad, useful or harmful. Expressed in the language of the oldest—the oral—instinctual impulses, the judgment is: 'I should like to eat this', or 'I should like to spit it out'; and, put more generally: 'I should like to take this into myself and to keep that out'. [. . .] As I have shown elsewhere, the original pleasure-ego wants to introject into itself everything that is good and eject from itself everything that is bad'.[20]

Without knowing it, Freud limits himself here to resuming and circumscribing an analogy proposed by Aristotle: 'What affirmation and negation are in the sphere of thought, pursuit and avoidance are in desire.'[21] But is it really the case that the negative judgement is a continuation by other means of spitting, keeping out, or avoiding? There is nothing in the nature of such a judgement that would make us think so. On the other hand, there are many indications that it opposes its archaic counterparts (as already happens in the case of repression). That is, there are many indications that one of the eminent prerogatives of negation is precisely that of

---

19 Freud, 'Negation', p. 236.

20 Ibid., pp. 236–7.

21 Aristotle, *Nicomachean Ethics*, 1139a, 21–2.

hindering, or at least postponing, the implementation of the non-linguistic gestures of refusal and subtraction. The two couples of which Aristotle speaks, affirmation/negation and pursuit/avoidance, do not proceed in parallel, mirroring each other from afar, but intersect: negation, a component of verbal thought, is able to block an avoidance, that is, the manifestation of desire that is most akin to it.

Freud himself offers some clues concerning the existence of a dissonance between the use of the sign 'not' and the drive-based rejection of unpleasant realities. When we read that 'affirmation—as a substitute [*Ersatz*] for uniting—belongs to Eros; negation—the successor [*Nachfolge*] to expulsion—belongs to the instinct of destruction,'[22] it is easy to notice the diversity of terms used to describe the two poles of judgement. While affirmation is the *Ersatz*, the derivative *alter ego* of the assimilating introjection, negation is rather the *Nachfolge*, the 'successor', or 'consequence', of the destructive ejection. What succeeds something else does not ever equate with it; the effect is never the exact copy of the cause from which it derives. Precisely insofar as it is not its *Ersatz*, or 'substitute', negation neatly distinguishes itself from a silent rebuff. But what is its role as *Nachfolge*? The real problem is attributing a determined content to the term 'consequence', which is as such very vague. In the same passage I have been commenting, Freud also writes: 'The creation of the symbol of negation has endowed thinking with a first measure of freedom [. . .] from the compulsion of the pleasure principle.'[23]

---

22 Freud, 'Negation', p. 239.

23 Ibid.

This should surprise us: the 'not' that a few lines above was a consequence of the pleasure principle, now becomes nothing less than the instrument with which thought liberates itself from it. Excluding the possibility that Freud was drunk, we need to ask how these two concomitant but discordant remarks on the function of negative judgements are connected and integrated. On closer inspection, when he observes that the 'not' breaks away from the pleasure principle, Freud is only specifying the meaning of the keyword *Nachfolge*. Negation is indeed the consequence of a drive, but a consequence whose fundamental characteristic is guaranteeing the speaker's independence from drives in general. The negative judgement induced by the desire for elimination or avoidance nonetheless enables us not to submit to this desire: hence, it enables us *not* to eliminate and *not* to avoid. The term 'consequence' is synonymous with 'reaction'. The construction of barriers that protect coastal areas follows from frequent sea storms; the installation of lightning conductors from thunderstorms: these consequences are reactions whose aim is to counter the phenomena that caused them. In turn, negation is the consequential reaction or the reactive consequence that mitigates and corrects the affective inclination to expel. It is a *Nachfolge* that targets its own premise, and neutralizes it: an effect that procures an antidote to the poison inherent to the corresponding cause.

There are two main ways in which negation jams the unfolding of destructive drives. The first, which I will call *homeopathic*, consists of the pure and simple translation of the will to annihilate the harmful alien into a negative statement. Pre-linguistic aggressiveness produces an *exclusion*: by spitting or killing, the psychic subject irrevocably separates himself from the object he opposes. On the contrary, the negative statement *includes* in itself the event or state of affairs it rejects. Moreover, it could not do so if it did not include it or, better, if it did not formulate it with great precision. When we say 'I cannot bear Giovanni's behaviour,' we still speak about Giovanni's behaviour, we preserve it at the centre of our thoughts, and, without being aware of it, we even spark the possibility of bearing it (just as when we say 'Mario is not at home,' we inevitably allude to the possibility that Mario is at home). Far from cancelling once and for all an unpleasant reality, the negative statement incorporates it, names it and provides a description of it. The semantic preservation of the 'evil' not only takes distance from its physical or psychological expulsion but also prevents it. The *Nachfolge* of the desire for spitting restrains spitting. The inclusionary refusal typical of negation hinders or at least suspends the exclusionary refusal dictated by the drive. I call the second way in which negation reacts to its non-verbal antecedent *polemical*. The independence of the sign 'not' from 'the compulsion of the pleasure principle' is at times carried out through the frontal opposition of the 'not' to what, within this principle, appeared to announce it—the inclination to chase away the unwanted thing. What is linguistically repelled is the destructive drive as such: 'I do not spit;' 'I do not attack the unbearable Giovanni;' 'I do not run away, although I am tempted.' It is important to consider that, even in this second case, negation preserves and highlights what it suppresses. While the statement 'I cannot bear Giovanni's behaviour' includes in itself the *object* that causes revulsion, that is, Giovanni's behaviour, the statements 'I do not spit,' 'I do not attack,' 'I do not run away' include in themselves, and even display, the *drive* to spit, attack and run away that, on the other hand, they inhibit. The grammatical first person can neutralize the intention to cancel and expel, by which it is actually possessed, only on condition of not cancelling or expelling it from the semantic content of its discourse.

It is certainly legitimate to question my interpretation of this part of Freud's essay. However, those who wish to do so would have to find out an alternative explanation for three glorious mysteries: why the negative judgement is a 'consequence' and not a 'substitute' of the innate tendency to distance ourselves from what is unpleasant; how we should precisely understand the *Nachfolge*; how the idea that negation is the consequence of a drive can be reconciled with the (at-first-sight-incompatible) idea that negation decrees the independence of verbal thought from the drives. I wish them luck. I must also stress that these legitimate doubts and alternative explanations are in the end not so important. The theoretical hypothesis I have put forward, availing myself of Freud's text, would not change one bit were somebody to show me that it forsakes the genuine intentions of the author. I would continue to think, eventually against Freud, that the annulment of the drives is obstructed, and not prolonged, by semantic annulment; that the gap between verbal negation and psychosomatic expulsion becomes manifest precisely on the occasions when negation holds expulsion back; that the reorganization of our emotional life carried out by language does not occur where discourse presents itself as an *Ersatz* of an introjective-amorous affect, but only where discourse blocks the way to an excluding-aggressive affect, by resorting to the peculiar power of the sign 'not'.

(c) In a book that has been seminal in many ways, *The Divided City*,[24] Nicole Loraux investigates with the aid of anthropological and semiotic categories a crucial episode in the history of Athens: in 403 BCE, after having defeated the bloody oligarchy of the Thirty, the democrats forbade any recollection of the sorrows and abuses of power suffered by the opposition during the tyranny. The political atrophy of the psychic faculty of memory was accomplished by a specific linguistic act. Every citizen was invited to make an oath dominated by the symbol of negation: 'I will not recall my tragedies' (*ou mnesikakéso*). To sanction the end of the fratricidal conflict, the exiled who had come back home used a negative performative statement; those who proffered it carried out an action (the oath), but an action which obliged them *not* to carry out another action (remembering). When connected with the illocutionary force of the verb 'to swear', negation is a *stimulus to inhibit* (see 3.3). That is, it induces us to omit and desist, thus instituting an empty space in the texture of collective praxis. But what did the 'not' inserted in the promissory formula pronounced by the Athenians have to keep at bay? If it had been freely practised, remembrance would have stirred up the instinctive, and never fully eradicable, desire for vengeance. The stimulus to

---

24 Nicole Loraux, *The Divided City: On Memory and Forgetting in Ancient Athens* (Cambridge, MA: MIT Press / Zone Books, 2002[1997]).

inhibit, verbally produced by the negative oath, thus targeted a more original stimulus, independent from language: the emotional stimulus to retaliate. In 403 BCE, in the city of Athens, something was done with words in order to abstain from doing something that did not require words: killing those who had killed.

The oath not to recall past events is antipodal to the physiological forgetting that is encouraged by the inevitable vanishing of memory. The performative statement 'I swear not to recall my tragedies' is the clear proof that the wrongs committed by the oligarchs have not been forgotten or, even less, forgiven. Used to inhibit the *act of remembering* and the related drive to revenge, negation nonetheless confers maximum visibility to both: the necessity to place an obstacle in their way sufficiently shows how obstinate and pressing that act and that drive are. The same applies to the *content of the memory*; the tragedies not to be remembered are explicitly mentioned in the oath imposed by the democrats, and thus remain obvious to the entire city. What should be kept silent is clearly said at the moment when it is interdicted. The empty space in the texture of collective praxis, instituted by the 'not' that incites the omission, certainly does not go unnoticed; on the contrary, it draws attention to itself and turns out to be far more conspicuous than any full space; it cannot be forgotten.

Insofar as negation preserves and exhibits the thought or desire it opposes, in the statement 'I will not recall the tragedies' there is always the possibility that, sooner or later, the tragedies will nonetheless be recalled, retaliation will take place and the city will again be wrecked by conflict. The aggressive drive is only suspended, and never abolished, by the use of the sign 'not'. This is a fragile, controversial, and hence temporary suspension. Given that the memory of the wrongs one suffered cannot be deleted: 'It should be neutralized without being completely lost: it should be domesticated by being installed, defused, indeed turned against itself. Thus, by the will of Athena, the Erinyes proclaim that they renounce their fury.'[25]

But everyone knows that, although they have agreed to become Eumenides, the Erinyes are at all times ready to assume again their ancient evil aspect. The civilizing metamorphosis that they underwent at the end of the trial against the matricide Orestes is always reversible. The 'not' that enabled that metamorphosis marks at the same time its abiding reversibility. It marks it and, in some cases, solicits it, even becoming its agent. I am referring to the cases in which negation is recursively applied to a previous negative statement: 'not (not *p*)'; in other words, to refer back to the events studied by Loraux, 'it is *not* that I will *not* recall the tragedies.' Double negation implies the *disinhibition* of the hunger for revenge. With just a hint of pedantry, it would be better to say: it implies a second and more complex inhibition, whose task is to silence the stimulus to inhibit further violence which the oath not to recall introduced in Athens. If the Eumenides are without doubt linguistic creatures, generated by the restraining retroaction of negation on destructive affects, the returning Erinyes can themselves at times be linguistic; these are the Erinyes that appear at the end of a temporal interval in which their

25 Ibid., p. 163.

conduct was characterized by benevolence, that is, the Erinyes as former Eumenides, the repenting Eumenides.

5.6
DESTROYING EMPATHY

When we examine the role of negation in the emotional vicissitudes of our species, it is necessary to fully take into account the changing ways in which negation *appears* to those who use it. It is not only the logical requisites of the 'not' that orchestrate the score of affects, but also the speaker's representation of them. When we proffer a negative statement about the pain that engulfs us, or the pleasure that consumes us, we can always believe to be doing something different from what we are really doing. The hypothetical misunderstanding of our own linguistic act itself has an emotional value. It is the very *use* of negation that feeds the fallacious appearances that emerge in relation to it. But it is still this *use* that enables us to refute, and then dissolve, these appearances. What is at stake is the progressive revelation of the nature and powers of the 'not' within communicative praxis. This is a progressive but far from linear revelation that actually includes oscillations and bottlenecks. If at all possible, we should come up with a *phenomenology of the negating consciousness*, that is, a history of the successive stages the human animal goes through in order to fully grasp the functioning of discourses in which it occurs to it to say in detail how things are *not*. If it is true that negation modifies experience as a whole, it is also true that a specific *experience of negation* befalls us. Those with some spare time should make sure they deal with it.

In the previous section, I have tried to outline the two initial stages of a hypothetical phenomenology of the negating consciousness. I now sum up its key aspects, in order to pave the way for a further and decisive quest.

(1) In the beginning, the speaker conceives negation as an equivalent or corollary to the multiple forms of non-linguistic annulment: repression, rejection, psychological expulsion, escape, material erasure, etc. Thus he does not acknowledge the specific prerogatives of the 'not'. But, although unknown to the speaker, these prerogatives already qualify his concrete linguistic activity. We therefore obtain a considerable discordance between the intention of the one who negates (let us say, the will to separate oneself from a detested object) and the result achieved by negating. This discordance is very similar to that tearing apart 'sense-certainty' in Hegel's *Phenomenology*.[26] While it is convinced that it denotes an individual object with the pronoun 'this', or an unrepeatable instant with the adverb 'now', 'sense-certainty' is proved wrong by the very words it uses; in fact, it quickly realizes that 'this' can refer to any object, and 'now' can refer to any instant. In the same way, a speaker who identifies the act of negating with a curettage or a combustion is blatantly contradicted by the 'not' he uses, since it leaves intact, and even evidences, the semantic content on which it intervenes. When we use negative statements to distance ourselves from an unpleasant reality, the tools we trust play tricks on us, since, in uttering these statements, we always remain in strict contact with what we wanted to avoid.

---

26 Hegel, *Phenomenology of Spirit*, pp. 58–66.

(2) The way in which negation *appears* to us, that is, the experience we have of it, changes radically as soon as we start to use it to block or mitigate the non-linguistic annulment of a certain state of affairs. That is to say, as soon as we happen to say: 'I do not expel,' 'I do not attack,' 'I do not destroy.' The fact that a negative statement is not the echo of a spit or escape is proved beyond reasonable doubt by the fact that it often manages to inhibit the gestures of spitting and escaping. From a phenomenological standpoint, it is necessary that negation oppose in praxis its supposed predecessors so as to bring to light the genetic and functional heterogeneity that distances it from them. It is only at this point that the speaker learns the distinctive characters of the logical operation that he has already carried out countless times without problems. The practical epiphany of the requisites of negation removes, even on a psychological level, previously cherished psychologistic illusions. But this epiphany is certainly not the point of arrival of a phenomenology of the negating consciousness. It opens the way instead to shattering and disquieting developments.

Freeing itself from false ancestors and surreptitious doubles, the syntactic connective 'not' gains an almost unlimited freedom of action. Its use is no longer bound to a particular emotional state, to circumscribed and foreseeable events, and to a well-defined set of triggering causes. The use of this connective becomes mobile and pervasive, and now concerns any emotional content. The detachment from the sad passions, caused by the negative statements that prevent their unfolding, is virtually extended to all passions. Having contrasted and paralysed the non-linguistic affects from which it appeared to derive (refusal, disgust, hostility, etc.), negation can contrast and paralyse any other affect—also and above all the affects that a psychologist would locate at its antipodes: amorous fusion, friendship, empathy, solidarity, the inclination to collaborate with one's peers. To put it with Freud, having inhibited the drive to exclude, to which it seemed related, the act of negating is certainly also able to inhibit the further drive to welcome and introject. Having settled accounts with what is similar prepares it for influencing what is alien. The animal that speaks, which thanks to the use of the 'not' restrained the aversion for the enemy, does not hesitate to restrain in the same way the sympathy that unites him with his travelling companions. Negation thus involves the whole spectrum of joyful feelings of which affirmation is the *Ersatz*, the 'substitute'. And it involves it not because it is in turn the *Ersatz* of destructive feelings but, on the contrary, because it polemically reacted to them, reducing and containing them. The new stage of the phenomenology of the negating consciousness is the one in which, whether timidly or arrogantly, the speaker manages to verify that any affective affirmation (that 'belongs to Eros', according to Freud) is always liable to negation.

The attraction for somebody or something is turned into an affirmative statement, and assumes the appearance of a verbal assent. But the affirmative statement can be contradicted at any time by the 'not'. Negating it, we undermine or freeze the attraction (or the empathy, the solidarity, etc.) that it embodied. At this stage, the speaker experiences the *relationship* between affirmation and negation. Thus, he has to deal with both poles taken together.

In this practical-emotional experience of the collision of A and not-A, he takes possession of an important logical truth. He retraces in his own way paths already beaten in the history of philosophy. In accordance with Aristotle,[27] the speaker discovers once again that the relationship between affirmation and negation ('Luca loves Sara,' 'Luca does not love Sara') has nothing in common with the conflict between two contrary notions (sweet and bitter, good and bad, etc.), or with the turning of a possession into a privation (blindness that takes the place of sight). In accordance with Kant's 'Attempt to Introduce the Concept of Negative Magnitudes into Philosophy', the speaker personally notices the unbridgeable distance that divides the couple affirmation/negation from the 'real opposition', that is, from the clashing of two forces that are as such positive, independent from each other, and each endowed with particular characteristics (the wind blocked by a mountain; the pain for the loss of one's mother that weakens the pleasure caused by the birth of a son, etc.). However, we should better understand why this *phenomenological repetition* of crucial episodes of theoretical philosophy occurs precisely when negation is applied to an affirmative statement that condenses in itself attraction, that is, the desire for inclusion and sharing.

The 'not' harms or softens the feeling of attraction expressed by the affirmative statement. But, in harming or softening it, it does not give voice to the symmetrical feeling of repulsion. Negating love does not mean replacing it with hatred. If this were the case, we would be confronted with a 'real opposition' between two autonomous

---

27 Aristotle, *Categories*, 11b17–13b35.

emotional tendencies, or with the relentless conflict into which contrary passions fall. But this is not the case. The speaker has soon ascertained that the act of negating is not the verbal counterpart of destructive feelings. He has ascertained it in his own praxis, since he had occasion several times to use the 'not' to defuse repulsion and silence hatred. Negation, which now influences inclusive friendship, cannot be confused with the official representative of the expulsive aversion that, on other occasions, it was equally able to influence. Being neither the means of a 'real opposition' (as is nausea when it eliminates hunger), nor a contrary doomed to take the place of its direct rival (as is bitterness in competition with sweetness), the negative statement revolves around the same affect which the corresponding affirmative statement deals with: it certainly refutes the latter, yet without delineating an alternative semantic content. The 'not' suspends the feeling of attraction but does not replace it with a heterogeneous feeling. The outcome is non-attraction, that is, a blocked attraction, which nevertheless remains what it is, and does not turn into something else. Negation is free, that is, mobile and pervasive, precisely because it does not take root in an emotional state that is different from the negated one. Its inclination to *suspend without replacing* enables it to function without limits: with respect to joy as much as with respect to rancour. 'Real opposition' and the war between contrary feelings are rare, or in any case take shape only on certain conditions: the simultaneous presence of pain and pleasure, or the actual mixing of resentment and tenderness directed at the same person, are essential. On the other hand, since it does not aim at replacing what it suspends, negation can be carried out in any context and at any time, with respect to any emotional mood. The speaker, who in his phenomenological itinerary reached Aristotle's and Kant's self-same conclusions after a series of attempts and errors, now knows inside out the freedom enjoyed by the 'not'; this freedom is more than sufficient to irrevocably distinguish it from physical clashes and psychological tensions. The speaker knows that by using this syntactic connective he can even derail the solidarity and the propensity for cooperation that nonetheless continue to inspire him.

The use of negation generates a kind of destructiveness far more intense and diffuse than that which issues from pre-linguistic drives. While the silent desire to expel resides in certain typical circumstances, and is aroused by contingent motives, the suspension of harmony and benevolence accomplished by the 'not' opens the door to a violence that is stateless, ubiquitous and polyvalent. The linguistic inhibition of the natural empathy among members of the same species does not need pretexts: it can occur at any time. The passage from instinctual aggressiveness to the aggressiveness that hinges on negation has something in common with the evolutionary transformation of mating. The latter is no longer periodical, that is, confined to the season when the animal is in heat, and becomes permanent, unforeseeable because always dormant. In the same way, the verbal sabotage of hospitality and friendship is always latent and hence unforeseeable. Those who stop at the second stage of the phenomenology of the negating consciousness—that in which the 'not' keeps repulsive hostility at bay—are satisfied with telling once again the comforting yet hackneyed tale of an intellect dedicated to putting a leash of words on animal behaviours. There is nothing less true and more nonsensical. What unleashes a specifically human bestiality is instead the supposed leash, that is to say, a thought wholly permeated by syntax. Negation's clamping down on the various kinds of physical or psychological, that is, non-linguistic, annulment is only the background for a disastrous collapse of social cooperation made possible by negation itself. What, on the one hand, negation protects is, on the other, even more endangered by it. The shelter provided by the 'not' has the singular characteristic of multiplying and magnifying dangers.[28]

---

28 In *Origins of Human Communication* (Cambridge, MA: MIT Press, 2008), Michael Tomasello claims that verbal language is embedded in the 'cooperative infrastructure', that is, in the inclination to collaborate and help that already animates the ostensive and mimicking gestures of primates. To understand what a pointed finger indicates, or what emotions are manifested by an alarmed or imploring physiognomy, we need to give importance to the same events, have comparable preoccupations and expectations, and pursue similar aims. That is, we need a 'joint attention'. Tomasello is right in supposing that 'arbitrary' languages would never have emerged without the 'cooperative infrastructure' inserted in gestural communication. He is also right in observing that, although they are more ductile and efficient, statements often do what was previously done by expressions of indication and physiognomic expressions: requesting something that may help us; informing those present about what may favour or interest them; sharing attitudes and feelings. But Tomasello is wrong when he concludes that verbal language greatly enhances empathy and the inclination to share that made language possible. He is wrong when he writes: 'Like many cultural products, human languages may in their turn

The failure of reciprocal recognition among animals endowed with language is a catastrophe that is ascribable only to negation. I have discussed this extensively in the first chapter of the book. Let us recall some essential points. The mirror neurons establish a dense network of intersubjective relations long before differentiated and self-conscious subjects are formed. I understand the actions and the emotions of another man because of the activation in my brain of the same neurons that would be activated if it were me carrying out those actions or feeling

---

contribute to further developments in the originating skills' (ibid., p. 343); 'human collaboration is the original home of human cooperative communication, but then this new form of communication facilitates ever more complex forms of collaboration in a coevolutionary spiral' (ibid., pp. 343–4). Negation, as a distinctive trait of 'arbitrary' languages, introduces a neat discontinuity with respect to ostensive and mimicking gestures. And, above all, it weakens emotional harmony and the propensity for mutual help implied by these gestures. The use of the 'not' opens the possibility of not helping, not informing, and not sharing. What is targeted by negative statements are not only the events and the emotional states that follow each other within the 'joint attentional frame', but also, at times, the permanence of such a 'frame'. The latter becomes itself ephemeral, uncertain and in need of confirmation. Contrary to what Tomasello thinks, the 'coevolutionary spiral' between intersubjective collaborations and verbal language always presupposes the possible collapse of the former by means of the latter. Being colonized by negation, discourses render frail and porous the 'cooperative infrastructure' on which they nonetheless rest. To put it very briefly: the 'not' promotes a social collaboration so refined, or so ambivalent, that it introjects the chronic crisis of collaboration.

those emotions. Thanks to the 'we-centric space'[29] that is
thereby instituted, I share from the beginning the experiences of my counterparts. More, I have the certainty that
these are living beings similar to me because I share their
experiences. Now, negation tears this 'we-centric space'
apart, weakening the harmony between members of the
same species that it ensured. Although the 'embodied
simulation' attests to the fact that the old suffering Jew
is a human primate, the Nazi officer does not hesitate to
say 'he is *not* a man.' The perceptive and neurophysiolo-
gical evidence is bracketed by a negative statement. How
do we explain this bracketing and the subsequent non-
recognition? The mirror neurons are an incontrovertible
biological apparatus. Unlike sweetness or whiteness, they
have no contrary, that is, there is no trace of a brain area
that foments incomprehension or extraneousness. Neither
are mirror neurons involved in a 'real opposition'; leaving
aside lesions, we do not know any physical force able to
annul their effects. The empathy caused by an incontrovertible biological apparatus can only be *suspended*, not
eliminated by something different that would replace it
entirely or in part. But this empathy can *always* be suspended. What determines the impasse of reciprocal recognition is indeed the logical operation that suspends every
semantic content without ever replacing it with another,
the logical operation that removes an emotional mood on
condition of preserving it. Moreover, the recognition of
the Jew as *Homo sapiens* is obstructed by the same 'not'
that inhibited—but certainly did not cancel—the aggressiveness inherent to our instincts. To be clear, this is the

---

29 Gallese, 'Neuroscienza delle relazioni sociali', p. 13.

same 'not' that rebutted the desire for vengeance that the Athenian democrats no doubt had when, in 403 BCE, they came back from exile after the end of the tyranny of the Thirty. The statement 'he is not a man,' uttered by the Nazi officer in spite of the persistent activity of mirror neurons, benefits from the same properties of negation that allowed the sedation, through the oath 'I will not recall my tragedies,' of the obvious impulse to repress the former repressors. Precisely because it is able to contain rancour and hostility, the linguistic animal is also able to disintegrate intra-specific empathy, up to the point of not recognizing its neighbours.

We know that the transformation of the belligerent Erinyes into sympathetic Eumenides is only provisional and reversible. Aggressiveness, which is inhibited or mitigated by the 'not', can be awakened following a second 'not', which revokes the pacifying outcome of the first. Inversely, the disavowal of another man, realized through negation, can in turn be negated. In the case of the Erinyes, double negation reawakens homicidal fury; in the case of a failed recognition, it heals a lesion suffered by empathy and restarts social cooperation. The field of affects is regulated by the oscillation between negation and the negation of negation, hence by the alternation between 'not p' and 'not (not p)'. In the concrete emotional experience of a speaker, both benevolence and hostility are never immediate, since they presuppose the paralysis of what could have paralysed them. Devoid of any cognitive relevance, the negation of negation (see Appendix B) is a specific linguistic *action*: like praying, threatening, promising, etc. When we use it, we do not placidly describe the world, but *do* something: for example, we renew a broken friendship, or restart a civil war after a long armistice. There is one important addition. Double negation, as a speech act, does not reactivate the initial affirmation: 'not (not p)', which is responsible for the deactivation of 'not p', also distances itself from 'p'. Having previously experienced the condition of Eumenides, the returning Erinyes are no longer pre-linguistic drives but personify the destructive power [*potenza*] of verbal thought. Similarly, standing out from the background of its possible failure, the accomplishment of reciprocal recognition among human animals does not mark a return to the original harmony automatically produced by mirror neurons, but wholly depends on the political power [*potenza*] of language; it is the always precarious result of the pacts and insurrections that punctuate the public sphere.

APPENDICES

A. NEGATIVE ACTIONS

Human praxis is to a large extent composed of actions that amount exclusively to *not* doing something. Here is a concise list: omitting, abstaining, avoiding, renouncing, disobeying, neglecting, hesitating, differing, keeping a secret, tolerating. Whether what is at stake is a general strike, a collective game or even the ordinary functioning of an institution, it is easy to acknowledge that there are multiple gestures that are not carried out—and hence remain inconspicuous—and as such accompany and corroborate the gestures we can observe. Not-doing not only mixes with doing but, in many cases, is even its inescapable presupposition. When we make an alliance, it is necessary to *avoid* accounting for the blows our new friend delivered in the past. To win a poker game, I often (reluctantly) need to *give up on* verifying whether my opponent who bets exorbitant sums of money is bluffing. In Hegel's *Phenomenology of Spirit*, it is history itself that is originated from desisting: the feral fight between two independent individuals, each of whom demands to be recognized by the other, becomes a relevant episode, open to tumultuous and unpredictable developments, only when one of the contenders *abstains* from continuing the battle all the way to its most extreme implications, and, instead, provisionally submits himself to the rival.

Negative actions are not a symptom of psychosomatic weakness. Those who carry them out demonstrate a unique alacrity. The doctor who disobeys the governmental order to report illegal immigrants in need of treatment is not indolent but indefatigable. A renunciation requires initiative, abundant energies, even obstinacy. Far from marking the collapse of praxis, omissions and abstentions are part of its framework. Or, better, they determine the caesurae, the pauses and the voids that allow praxis to have a framework. Unlike instinctual behaviour, which does not know empty spaces, praxis always includes in itself a certain quota of *untimeliness*, that is, a multitude of intentional non-implementations. Negative actions, which are mostly interstitial and disseminated across every day of our lives, nevertheless do not fail to characterize, thanks to their unusual concentration, a particular field of experience, a ritual or a biography. Let me give you some examples. Taboo is a cohesive and consistent system of omissions. In ancient Rome, the high priest of Jupiter, the *Flamen Dialis*, had to comply with a set of obligations enunciated by a series of 'nots': not riding a horse, not wearing a ring that is not broken, not having a knot on any part of his garments, not touching a dead body, not being uncovered in the open air, etc.[1] Moreover, it is well known that ascetic practices aim at reducing the activity of the Ego, nurturing a state of lasting suspension. Simon Weil wrote: 'The soul, like a gas, tends to occupy the whole of the space left open to it [. . .] Not to exercise all the power at one's disposal is to endure the void [. . .] Evil consists in action, good in non-action or non-active action.'[2]

The *amor vacui*, brought to the limit in taboo-precepts and asceticism, has a profane, and at times euphoric, extension in contemporary forms of life, characterized as they are by an inflexible flexibility and by the habit of not cultivating solid habits. The intimate relation with a myriad of simultaneous and incompatible possibilities has generated a diffuse inclination to abstain, avoid and differ; the risk that the acts we carry out may exclude those that are latent or virtual—for which we need to remain constantly available—is too big. Pronounced actions that univocally identify us, and, worse, do so once and for all, are taboo. In the job market and in the communication made available by new technologies, a strange species of ascetic lurks: experts in 'non-active actions', determined not to compromise their immaculate potentiality [*potenza*] with accurate and circumscribed actuations [*attuazioni*].

---

1 Sigmund Freud, *Totem and Taboo* in James Strachey (ed.), *The Standard Edition of the Complete Psychological Works of Sigmund Freud, Volume 13* (London: Vintage, 2001[1913]), pp. 1–162; here, p. 46.

2 Simone Weil, *The Notebooks of Simone Weil* (Abingdon: Routledge, 2004), p. 198, p. 163, p. 127.

Although they are certainly frequent and incisive, negative actions preserve an enigmatic physiognomy. First of all, one wonders whether it is correct to pass them off as authentic actions. Is *not* doing something itself a doing that is liable to descriptions, filled with memorable events, exposed to successes and failures? Or are we in the presence of the pure and simple negation of doing as such? The answer of the only two authors who have dealt with this issue in depth—the Doctor of the Church, Thomas Aquinas, and the English analytic philosopher, Gilbert Rye—is uncertain and varying. In the *Quaestiones disputatae de malo* [Disputed Questions on Evil], when he tries to define the nature of the sins of omission, Aquinas observes that they do not require an independent act, and are fully resolved in the absence of the right act. Yet shortly after he adds that *sub facere includitur etiam non facere*, 'even deeds not done are included in deeds,'[3] since omission would in turn be a kind of activity. In the essay entitled 'Negative "Actions"' (1973), Ryle shows that he shares Aquinas' hesitation (he probably knew the latter's text on the sins of omission). In spite of the fact that they are rich of consequences, and hence open to praise or reproach, renunciation and abstention are in many decisive ways different from acting as normally understood: they do not need materials or tools; they do not presuppose a specific ability; above all, they do not have their own content. In the end:

> Our negative 'actions' seem not to qualify as actions proper, for the reason that the full story

---

3 Thomas Aquinas, *On Evil* (Oxford: Oxford University Press, 2003), p. 94.

of a positive action would report it with its full complement of chronological, behavioural, technical, circumstantial (etc.) details, while the full story of a negative 'action' would be specific only about the particular thing that the agent did *not* do.[4]

If Aquinas and Ryle strongly doubt that omission, abstention, disobedience, renunciation, etc., are actions, it is because they acknowledge the strict similarity between these different types of not-doing and linguistic negation. Aquinas writes that *omissio negatio quedam est*, 'omission is a negation.'[5] Ryle admits that the theme that interests us 'is nothing more than an application to a familiar point about negation in general'.[6] Let us consider why, when it faithfully conforms to the functioning of the 'not', an omission seems to lose every right to be considered a genuine action. The statement 'Aldo is not at home' only says where Aldo is not, without specifying in what other place he is; in the same way, the omission of a charitable gesture does not replace it with an aggressive or libidinous gesture, but limits itself to not carrying it out. Just like negation does not introduce a new meaning, so omission, which is the practical correlate of negation, does not give rise to a new action. This is a misleading equation, which I would like to refute. Let me be clear: Aquinas and Ryle are entirely correct in stressing the isomorphism between the logical requisites of negative statements and the

---

4 Gilbert Ryle, 'Negative "Actions"', *Hermathema*, 115 (1973), pp. 81–93; here, p. 84.

5 Aquinas, *On Evil*, p. 90.

6 Ryle, 'Negative "Actions"', p. 84.

manifold ways in which we do not do something. But, looking more closely, it is precisely this isomorphism that suggests that not-doing constitutes a fundamental element of praxis. Not revealing the names of our comrades in arms even when the cops electrocuted our genital organs was an all-round *action*; and, moreover, it was such not because that silence was alien to the faculty of negation, but, on the contrary, because it introjected its distinctive traits.

Aquinas and Ryle's mistake lies in reducing the omission of a charitable gesture and renouncing to go out with a friend to the linguistic account of their effects, that is, to sentences such as 'he has not helped the derelicts' and 'he is not going out with his friend any more.' These sentences, analogous in all ways to 'Aldo is not at home,' make us believe that nothing happens when we omit or renounce. The sore point is that, in spite of accurately representing the 'particular thing that the agent did *not* do', they do not provide any information on the nature of not-doing. But what aspires to the rank of an action is only the not-doing, and certainly not its outcome, that is, the not-done. In order not to overlook the aspect that really matters, it is necessary to follow a different path. Omission and renunciation should not be equated to negation as a final *result*, an expressive product or *dictum*, but to negation as a logical *operation*, a semantic work or *actio dicendi*. The not-doing has little in common with what is communicated by the assertion 'Aldo is not at home,' whereas it shares a lot with the tortuous trajectory the speaker has to go through in order to formulate it. If we really wished at all costs to indicate a verbal counterpart of our abstentions and withdrawals, we would have to abandon the object-language ('Aldo is not at home,' for example) and use a metalinguistic statement such as 'I use negation to dispel the opinion that Aldo is at home;' the latter's advantage is that it exhibits the pragmatic profile of denial, that is, its character as an operation and even as an event. The not-doing is not a suspended implementation but the *act* of suspending a given implementation without replacing it with something else. It would be unreasonable to claim that when we say 'Giovanni is a traitor,' inasmuch as we talk about something that is not, we are not really talking. We will recall that this is the sophist's fallacious hypothesis, which in Plato's dialogue is opposed with excellent arguments by the Stranger and Theaetetus. But it would be equally unreasonable, and even sophistic, to claim that when we omit or renounce, inasmuch as we are not carrying out any action that is alternative to the one we neglected, we are not really acting.

To clarify the structure of negative actions (which are all-round actions, emancipated from the weakening inverted commas that Ryle adopts in their case), we therefore need to examine negation as an *operation*. As we have already discussed it several times in this book, I only propose a short summary of this operation. The *actio negandi* roughly involves three stages.

We go back from the affirmative assertion 'Aldo is at home'—uttered by somebody or merely hypothetical—to the neutral meaning around which it revolves, 'Aldo's being at home', which, as independent from the environmental matters of fact and from psychological representations, remains open to both assent and denial.

We then convert the neutral meaning 'Aldo's being at home' into the modal statement 'it is possible that Aldo is at home and, thus, also that he is *not* at home'; this clearly attests to the meaning's detachment from empirical data and, more in general, from the present.

We finally actualize the 'possible that he is not' as an integral part of the formula 'it is possible that he is and that he is not,' and obtain in this way the negative assertion 'Aldo is not at home.'

Let us now return to the not-doing, that is, the act of suspending an implementation without replacing it with anything different. The omission of the charitable gesture and giving up on meeting a friend follow the first two stages, (a) and (b), of the operation that produces a negative assertion, but not the third. More precisely: the not-doing absorbs the last stage of the *actio negandi* into the second; it combines (b) and (c) rendering them almost indiscernible. If it is transposed onto praxis, the logical procedure that permeates negation undergoes an abrupt contraction. To be convinced of this, we only need to take a close look at what happens when we abstain or desist.

Omission and renunciation start off by carving out the neutral meaning of an action that, for the most various reasons (habits, prescriptions, advantages), presents an overt affirmative tone—that is, it is a task that we perform since it seems natural, correct or convenient. The neutral meaning of the action, for example, 'helping the derelicts' or 'going out with a friend', is always equidistant from doing and not-doing. Omission and renunciation therefore bring the action back to its state of mere possibility: 'It is possible to help and not to help the derelicts;'

'It is possible to go out and not to go out with a friend.'
Yet, portraying the action to be carried out as an eventuality that is still unprejudiced means *not* carrying it out.
This is the crux of the matter: the equidistance between
doing and not-doing, inherent to neutral meaning, already
implies as such the prevalence of not-doing. While in
verbal communication the modal statement 'it is possible
that p and that not p' remains neatly distinct from the
negative assertion 'not p', since it is its logical antecedent,
in praxis we instead have a complete overlapping of the
two moments. A possible action is only an action that is
not carried out; but not carrying out an action amounts
to negating it; hence, the possibility of an action is
unveiled precisely when we negate it and, reciprocally,
the negation of an action fully amounts to unveiling its
possibility. Keeping a secret is not different from dwelling
for a short or long time on the threshold where it is
possible to reveal it or not. When we desist from the habit
of waking up at five in the morning, we restore the situation in which we can both wake up or not wake up at
such an abominable hour.

The condensation between the syntactic connective
'not' and the modal functor 'it is possible that' acquires its
utmost evidence in the case of *deferral* and *hesitation*. It
would be useless and even slightly funny to ask whether,
in differing or hesitating, we do not do action y because
we protract its possibility, or, on the contrary, we protract
the possibility of action y because we do not do it. A
peremptory option for one of the two alternatives not
only does not prevent an equally peremptory option for
the other, but even requires it. Deferral and hesitation are

the privileged abode of dispositional adjectives, whose identification symbol is the suffix 'able' (see 3.6): the object to be enjoyed becomes enjoy*able*; the book to be read read*able*; the boss to be contrasted contrast*able*, etc. But the transformation of enjoyment into enjoy*ability*, of reading into read*ability*, of contrast into contrast*ability*, realized by the demanding actions of differing and hesitating, involves the negation of enjoying, reading, contrasting, that is to say, their suspension without replacement. Lingering on the 'able', we do *not* do something precisely to the extent to which we prospect its possibility.

Finally, let me add a couple of words about the temporal articulation of negative actions. Omissions and renunciations interweave timeliness with untimeliness; they articulate a 'now' that nonetheless opens the door to the 'not now'. They are well-defined occurrences, whose presence is inscribed without difficulty on the calendar; they start, and at times finish, on a verifiable date. But their *duration*, that is, the 'while' or 'in the meantime' in which omission and renunciation are valid, shies away from chronological subdivisions. Within this duration, we are unable to individuate a before and an after, a past and a future, that is, a development. Exactly two months ago, we have desisted from assaulting the Ministry of the Treasury and from courting a graceful person. But what happened to our twofold desistence from that moment on? Although it never failed, it has ceased to coincide with any kind of 'now'. A clock without hands has been registering its persistence. It would be absurd to say that last Saturday, and again yesterday, in addition to working, getting drunk, playing tennis, we abstained yet again from

assaulting and courting. The duration of a negative action
is a 'not now' in which presence is eclipsed. For an intuitive reason: two months ago, the act of desisting suspended the endeavour of assaulting the Ministry of the
Treasury because it confined it to the region of the possible. Or better, because it returned to the neutral meaning
'assaulting the Ministry of the Treasury', which, being
open to both doing and not-doing, always remains
untimely, or, indeed, potential. The 'while' or 'in the
meantime', in which to date we have continued to desist,
is the temporal counterpart of the modal statement 'it is
possible both to assault and not to assault the Ministry.'
The possible is never present; it eludes calendars; it knows
neither succession nor simultaneity. The duration of
desistence is therefore filled by the enduring untimeliness
of the possible (or, which is the same, by the no less enduring untimeliness of meaning separated from denotation).

Negative actions, which are as such datable, inject the
'not now' at the heart of praxis. They are real acts whose
point of arrival is the exhibition of a possibility—without
doubt a hypnotic and paralysing possibility. But the
untimeliness or 'not now', which is the *goal* of omissions
and renunciations, also constitutes the hidden *premise* of
affirmative actions. The assault on the Ministry of the
Treasury arises from the possibility of assaulting and not
assaulting it. That is, it originates from the same neutral
meaning 'assaulting the Ministry of the Treasury' upon
which our previous desistence conclusively dwelt. The
temporal lacunae that deferrals and hesitations establish
in a life or in a revolution are the phenomenal manifestation of that untimeliness/potentiality in which we have

no problem recognizing the presupposition of acting in general. Therefore it is right to conclude that each affirmative action embodies in itself, as an *incipit* or an inescapable condition, its possible omission. The Paris Commune started from the void of presence, that is, the dateless 'not now', in which the renunciation to proclaim it would have culminated.

B. DOUBLE NEGATION: A RESOURCE FOR PRAXIS

During a melancholic or agitated conversation a woman says to the man she had up to then favoured: 'It is *not* that I do *not* love you.' Far from being flattered, he immediately grasps two philosophical truths. The first is that double negation never equates with the affirmation that it appears to stand in for. The logical and sentimental distance that separates the thorny 'it is not that I do not love you' from the reassuring 'I love you' is unbridgeable. As soon as it is introduced, the couple of consecutive 'noes' cannot be eliminated by translating it into a straight-forward 'yes': the statement 'not (not p)' has moved the axis of discourse, adumbrating a further meaning that is heterogeneous and often discordant from 'p'. The second philosophical truth the distressed man acquaints himself with is that the negation of a negation does not describe anything, and rather amounts to an *action*. Although it is parasitical and superfluous from a cognitive standpoint, 'It is not that I do not love you' has nonetheless a formidable pragmatic value. Rather than offering an account of an already delineated state of affairs, it establishes a new and unexpected one. The man does not ask himself whether the words he hears correspond to reality, but what the woman is *doing* by uttering them, that is, what kind of reality her speech act is producing. These two truths imply each other, and form a sort of circle. The semantic gap between 'not (not p)' and 'p' is no longer mysterious only if we recognize that saying 'not (not p)' is an action; vice versa, the action that is carried out by saying 'not (not p)' becomes intelligible only if we bear in mind the existence of a semantic gap between 'not (not p)' and 'p'.

Double negation modifies the basic meaning around which both a simple negation and a direct affirmation revolve (or could have revolved). The love we speak about in 'it is not that I do not love you' differs in some important ways from the one that is at stake both in the catastrophic 'I do not love you' and in the tender 'I love you' of the good old days. It is an affect in transformation, abounding with unprecedented undertones. While she denies that she does not love her partner, the woman however implies that it is difficult to love him as before—in a way that is dear to him. Altering the neutral sense 'loving you' dominant up to that point, double negation creates a curious *zone of indetermination* in which one neither fully refuses nor entirely accepts. We should pay attention to the use of the 'not' before negative adjectives.[1] When we say 'Pietro is not insincere,' 'Luisa is not unhappy,' 'The solution is not unconceivable,' we are not at all claiming that Pietro is actually sincere, Luisa really happy, and the solution definitely conceivable. We rather privilege an intermediate state between affirmation and negation, characterized by the temporary renunciation of both (hence by a 'neither . . . nor'). And it is precisely in this intermediate state, or zone of indetermination, that we experience a metamorphosis of the habitual meanings 'being sincere', 'being happy', being conceivable'—taken for granted up to that point.

Following a simile proposed by Wittgenstein (see 3.4), each meaning is an 'entire measuring stick', that is, a measuring instrument that supplies changing results on the different occasions in which it is applied. It rests with the affirmative and negative assertion to position the stick on a specific mark. Yet, when we have a double negation (such as 'I am not saying that Giovanna is not generous'), it is the 'entire measuring stick' (i.e. the semantic content 'being generous', as such open to opposite variations) that undergoes a more or less drastic change. The second 'not' provides a variation and redefinition of the measuring instrument that we previously used. Inasmuch as it modifies the neutral sense that is not yet qualified by a 'yes' or a 'no', the negation of a negation cannot at all be compared with a direct affirmation, which is instead based on this sense. In other words, the modification of the neutral sense is the *action* (comparable to an order, an oath, a verdict, etc.) that the speaker carries out when he turns to the

---

1 See Horn, *A Natural History of Negation*, pp. 296–308.

negation of a negation. In the end, it thus seems to me that it is not incorrect to ascribe the gap between 'it is not that I do not love you' and 'I love you' to the fact that the action realized by uttering the first statement would be neglected if we adopted the second. The two philosophical truths, reluctantly glimpsed by the lover when the woman tells him the fatal sentence, are different—yet in agreement and interchangeable—versions of one and the same event: the transformation of the 'entire measuring stick' by means of double negation.

We saw earlier (see 3.6) that the 'not' locates the state of affairs it confronts in the field of the possible. When we say 'I do not feel pain' we evoke our potential suffering; when we say 'Giorgio has not been kind,' we allude to the affable and caring behaviour that Giorgio could have displayed. This is obviously also valid in the case of double negation. But in its case it is the original negation, the one we are now committed to removing, that dons the robes of the possible. The sentence 'it is not that I do not love you' does exclude the tragedy that would be conveyed by 'I do not love you,' but in excluding it, it clearly ventilates its eventuality, and perhaps its imminence. The syntactic construction 'not (not p)' exhibits the *deniability* of 'p' precisely as it neutralizes it. But what is it that makes us use 'not (not p)'? If we wished to contradict 'not p', affirming 'p' would be enough. With double negation the speaker does something more complex and ambitious: he aims at creating a situation whereby 'not p', although it is possible, is nonetheless incongruous, trimmed, *ineffective*. The simple negation 'Giacomo is not courageous,' hinging on the current meaning 'being courageous', is annulled by the second negation, 'I am not saying that Giacomo is not courageous,' whose specific operation amounts to amplifying, distorting, or innovating the notion of courage. Having introjected the deniability of the initial semantic content, 'not (not p)' proposes this content again in an unusual acceptation, with respect to which 'not p'—by now similar to an archaic relic—can only sensationally fail.

These observations are still too reticent. Here is a less cautious paraphrase. Double negation is a *historical microcosm*. Between the two 'nots' there is always a temporal discrepancy, that is, an essential *diachrony*. To avoid any misunderstanding: I am not speaking of an interval that can be timed. It is not important whether the additional 'not' occurs months or years after since the occurrence of the first. It may, but that is irrelevant. What matters is that, for the sheer fact of being formulated, the second negation confines the first in a flat 'at that time', and posits itself as the 'after' in which it is judged and rejected. It is the *internal relation* between 'not p' and 'not (not p)' that is diachronic and historical. It reproduces on a very small scale the articulation of becoming. In the statement 'I am not saying that Giovanna is not generous,' the original negation, 'Giovanna is not generous,' is pushed back into the past, not because it was uttered a long time ago and then recognized as false, but because the further negation qualifies again the neutral sense 'being generous' on which the original negation rested. The second 'not' refutes the first on condition of rendering it *anachronistic*. Inscribing 'not p' in the field of the possible, 'not (not p)' keeps alive its *memory*. But 'not p', as the object of a memory, is preserved by 'not (not p)' as something *passed*, which *now* no longer has any operational bearing. The negation of communism becomes anachronistic, and precisely as such is in turn negated, as soon as the sense of 'communism' inherited from the twentieth century (the idolatry of the State apparatus; the glorification of the factory, etc.) is transformed at its roots by class struggles marked by a civilized contempt for wage labour and for that fringe gang, both marginal and ferocious, that goes by the name of State. The statement 'not (not communism)' embodies, and thus attests to and bequeaths, the deniability of communism, but in a way that makes it spin out of gear thanks to a semantic displacement of the concept in question.

Yearning for completeness, I add a secondary hypothesis, to which I feel attracted but also have some doubts about. Perhaps, there is another way in which the modification of the semantic content 'p' by means of 'not (not p)' can take place. Let us suppose that 'p' concerns a *contingent social behaviour*. The negative statement 'not p' refutes this behaviour. Let us now ask what are the effects of the negation of the first negation. Rather than rehabilitating the behaviour 'p' as it was, the second 'not' alters its sense. But what does this alteration precisely amount to? My hypothesis is that, in certain historically crucial circumstances (I think especially of riots, civil wars, and the state of exception), the negation of negation raises 'p' from its primitive identity as contingent behaviour to the rank of *rule*. In 1969, at the Mirafiori Fiat factory, the workers of the bodywork section chased away the timekeepers devoted to cutting down the time of production ('p', contingent behaviour); the company tried to erase the memory of this episode, returning those gentlemen to their place ('not p'); in the following years, the workers tolerated the presence of timekeepers provided that they remained prudently inactive; thanks to this peculiar 'not (not p)', the slowing down of the rhythm of production was no longer a sporadic event but a legislative principle. Given that it was still referring to 'p' as a contingent behaviour, 'not p' ended up biting the dust; it was 'not (not p)' that bestowed it an anachronistic aspect.

I repeat this point: thanks to the second 'not', the empirical fact becomes a normative criterion. And a normative criterion is, as such, never correct or incorrect, since it itself establishes the difference between correctness and incorrectness. According to Wittgenstein, there are facts of life, particular experiences, and consolidated habits that, from a certain moment, start to perform the function of rules; empirical propositions that, as time goes by, turn into grammatical propositions. In a passage of *On Certainty*, he writes: 'It might be imagined that some propositions, of the form of empirical propositions, were hardened and functioned as channels for such empirical propositions as were not hardened but fluid.'[2]

So, the passage from fluidity to rigidity, from the empirical to the grammatical, from the *quaestio facti* to the *quaestio juris* is marked by the negation of a previous negation. The temporal nature of this passage is evident: the contingent behaviour that *then* emerged *later* acquires the authority of a rule. The diachronic relation between the two 'nots', that is, the cornerstone of 'not (not p)', is the logical form most suited to the historical genesis of norms. But, as I was saying, this is only a secondary

---

2 Ludwig Wittgenstein, *On Certainty* (Oxford: Blackwell, 1969), p. 96.

hypothesis, still uncertain, which I will examine more carefully elsewhere.

Double negation is a fragment of praxis. It is the action with which the speaker suddenly innovates the semantic content underlying both a simple negation and a direct affirmation. Like any other action, double negation should not be considered as true or false, but as *successful* or *failed*. Following the terminology coined by Austin with regard to performative statements ('I open this session,' 'I swear that I will not take revenge,' 'I sentence the accused to twelve years in prison,' etc.) we could also say that 'not (not *p*)' is *felicitous* or *infelicitous*. For Austin, the performative statement 'I take this woman to be my lawfully wedded wife' turns out to be infelicitous— that is, it does not accomplish marriage—if some material conditions are missing, for instance, the presence of the fiancée, being a bachelor or being in the presence of a priest or a city councilman. Double negation is subjected to analogous constraints. The verbal action 'not (not *p*)' is *infelicitous*, i.e. defective, if it does not link with a set of non-verbal behaviours, events, emotions that allow it effectively to vary the neutral sense that has been in force until that moment. It is therefore infelicitous if it limits itself to coexisting with the possibility of the first negation, rather than decreeing its anachronism. In this case, the sequence of the two 'nots' is similar to a performative statement that is uttered as a joke or recited by an actor on a stage: it is vacuous, devoid of consequences. Double negation is thus reduced to a diplomatic expedient, a litotes, or a redundant substitute of direct affirmation. The success of 'it is not that I do not love you' depends to a large extent on a shortage of embraces, evasive gazes, and the discreet composure that all precede or accompany the sentence. And the *felicitousness* of 'not (not communism)' is ensured by the sequence of political conflicts that, far from restating it, overturn the original meaning of 'communism' to the point of defusing its previous negation. Although it is simply an action carried out by means of words, 'not (not p)' obtains its own efficacy from the dense network of non-linguistic actions that it both presupposes and elicits. Double negation, as a fragment of praxis, forms a *coalition* with countless heterogeneous fragments (yet without *describing* them); it is supported by silent activities, but, doing something they would not be able to do, it re-determines in turn their nature and destiny.